NATIONAL REAL ESTATE LICENSE EXAM PREP

Ace on the First Try. An Easy-to-Follow Study Guide, featuring 600 Expertly Explained Questions and Exclusive Tips Designed to Achieve a 99% Success Rate

Leo Mills

The purpose of this document is to furnish accurate and dependable information on the subject matter and issues addressed. It stems from a Declaration of Principles equally accepted and approved by both a Committee of the American Bar Association and a Committee of Publishers and Associations.

TABLE OF CONTENTS

EXTRA BONUSES

600+ EXPERTLY EXPLAINED QUESTIONS

-

TIPS FOR CAREER SUCCESS

-

DIGITAL FLASHCARDS

GO TO THE END OF THE BOOK AND SCAN THE QR CODE

INTRODUCTION

Congratulations on taking the first decisive step toward achieving your dream of becoming a licensed real estate professional! By choosing this guide, you've not only set yourself up for success on the exam but also for a flourishing career in real estate.

This book is crafted to guide you through the complexities of the real estate licensing exam with ease and confidence. With over 600 expertly explained questions, tailored tips for career success, and the use of digital flashcards, you hold the key to a comprehensive understanding of what it takes to excel.

As you turn each page, you will uncover the critical knowledge areas essential for your exam. The content is structured to build your understanding from the ground up, ensuring no stone is left unturned. Whether you are new to real estate or looking to solidify and expand your existing knowledge, this guide meets you where you are.

To enhance your learning experience, don't forget to download the exclusive bonuses included with your book purchase. These resources are designed to complement the material in the book and provide you with a well-rounded preparation experience.

Every chapter of this book is an opportunity to advance closer to your goal. I understand the challenges that come with preparing for the real estate exam and have developed this resource to make your study sessions as productive and engaging as possible.

So, let's get started! Prepare to immerse yourself in learning, practice rigorously, and walk into your exam with confidence. Your journey to becoming a licensed real estate agent starts now. Download your bonuses, set up your study space, and embark on your path to success.

Welcome to the first day of your promising career in real estate. Let's ace this together!

CHAPTER 1: GETTING STARTED

Exam Format and Structure Overview

The U.S. real estate licensing exam is a comprehensive assessment designed to evaluate the candidate's knowledge and understanding of real estate principles, practices, laws, and regulations. This exam is structured to cover a wide array of topics essential for a successful career in real estate. The format of the exam includes multiple-choice questions, which are divided into various sections, each focusing on a different aspect of real estate. These sections may include, but are not limited to, real estate principles and practices, property ownership and land use, valuation and market analysis, real estate financing, and law and ethics.

Candidates are required to answer a set number of questions within a specified duration, typically ranging from 3 to 4 hours. The exact number of questions and the time allotted can vary by state, as each state's real estate commission may set its own standards for the exam. The scoring criteria are also determined by the state, with most requiring a passing score of 70% or higher. It is crucial for candidates to familiarize themselves with the specific requirements of the state in which they intend to practice.

The exam's multiple-choice questions are designed to test the candidate's ability to apply knowledge in practical, real-world scenarios. Each question presents a situation or problem that a real estate professional might encounter, requiring the selection of the best answer from four options. This format assesses not only the candidate's factual knowledge but also their critical thinking and problem-solving skills.

For example, a sample multiple-choice question might be structured as follows:

What is the primary purpose of a title search in real estate transactions?

[A] To verify the seller's right to transfer ownership

[B] To determine the property's market value

[C] To inspect the property's condition

[D] To calculate property taxes due

Correct answer: [A] To verify the seller's right to transfer ownership.

Explanation: A title search is conducted to ensure that the seller has the legal right to transfer ownership of the property and that there are no liens, encumbrances, or other claims against the property that would impede the sale. This process is crucial for protecting the buyer's interests and ensuring a clear title is transferred.

Understanding the exam format and structure is vital for effective preparation. Candidates are encouraged to review practice exams and study materials that reflect the style and content of the actual exam. This approach helps in familiarizing oneself with the types of questions asked, the breadth of topics covered, and the strategic thinking required to select the correct answers. Additionally, time management is a critical skill during the exam, as candidates must pace themselves to ensure they have sufficient time to consider each question thoughtfully.

In preparation for the real estate licensing exam, candidates should focus on a comprehensive study plan that covers all sections of the exam, practice with sample questions to gain familiarity with the question format, and develop test-taking strategies that include time management and the process of elimination for challenging questions. By understanding the exam's format and structure and preparing accordingly, candidates can approach the exam with confidence, aiming to achieve a passing score on their first attempt.

CHAPTER 2: REAL ESTATE PRINCIPLES AND PRACTICES

Fundamentals of Real Estate

Property rights are a cornerstone of real estate transactions, granting individuals the legal authority to possess, use, and transfer land or buildings. These rights are protected by law, ensuring that property owners can control their assets within the confines of legal restrictions. Understanding property rights is essential for anyone entering the real estate field, as these rights define the scope of what owners can do with their property, from development to sale.

Types of ownership in real estate vary, offering different rights and responsibilities to property holders. Sole ownership, or tenancy in severalty, occurs when a property is owned by a single individual who has exclusive rights over it. Joint tenancy, on the other hand, involves two or more people owning property together, with rights of survivorship meaning that upon the death of one owner, their share automatically transfers to the surviving owner(s). Tenancy in common is another form of co-ownership where individuals share ownership of a property, but without rights of survivorship, allowing them to will their share to someone else upon death. Community property is a concept recognized in some states, referring to property acquired during marriage, which is considered owned equally by both spouses.

The legal definitions relevant to real estate transactions extend beyond property rights and types of ownership. They encompass a range of terms and concepts that are foundational to the practice of real estate. For example, the term "real property" refers to land and any permanent structures on it, distinguishing it from "personal property," which includes movable items like furniture or vehicles. "Easements" grant the right to use another's land for a specific purpose, such as a utility company laying cables, while "encumbrances" are claims or liens against a property that can affect its use and transferability.

Understanding these concepts is vital for real estate professionals who must navigate the complexities of property transactions, ensuring they operate within the bounds of the law while meeting their clients' needs. Whether dealing with sales, leases, or property management, a solid grasp of real estate principles lays the foundation for successful practice in the industry.

Exercise:

1. What type of ownership allows an owner's interest in the property to automatically transfer to the surviving owners upon their death?

[A] Sole ownership

[B] Joint tenancy

[C] Tenancy in common

[D] Community property

Correct answer: [B] Joint tenancy.

Explanation: Joint tenancy includes the right of survivorship, which means that when one of the owners dies, their interest in the property automatically passes to the surviving owner(s), without the need for probate.

2. Which term refers to movable items that are not considered part of real property?

[A] Easements

[B] Encumbrances

[C] Personal property

[D] Real property

Correct answer: [C] Personal property.

Explanation: Personal property includes movable items that are not attached to or part of the land or buildings, distinguishing it from real property, which includes the land and any permanent structures on it.

Exploring Land and Real Estate Distinctions

The distinctions between land, real estate, and real property are foundational to understanding the legal and practical nuances of property ownership and transactions in the real estate sector. Land refers to the earth's surface extending downward to the center of the earth and upward to infinity, including permanent natural objects such as trees and water. Real estate encompasses land and any man-made structures that are permanently attached to it, such as houses and buildings, making it a broader concept that includes both the physical ground and any additions. Real property, on the other hand, extends the definition of real estate to include the bundle of rights associated with the ownership of the land and buildings, such as the right to possess, use, sell, lease, and enjoy the property.

The characteristics of land include its immobility, indestructibility, and uniqueness. Each parcel of land is geographically unique, and its location plays a crucial role in determining its value. The legal implications of these characteristics are significant. For instance, the immobility of land necessitates the use of legal descriptions to accurately identify property boundaries and locations for transactions and records. The indestructibility of land ensures that it remains a valuable asset over time, which impacts economic decisions and development strategies. The uniqueness of each parcel of land means that real estate markets are highly localized, and property values can vary significantly even within short distances.

Understanding the distinctions between land, real estate, and real property is crucial for real estate professionals, as these concepts influence many aspects of the industry, from property valuation to legal documentation and zoning regulations. The rights associated with real property ownership, such as the right of exclusion, the right to sell or lease, and the right to occupy, are governed by a complex framework of laws and regulations that ensure the orderly conduct of real estate transactions and the resolution of disputes.

Exercise:

1. What distinguishes real property from real estate?

[A] The inclusion of natural objects

[B] The addition of man-made structures to the land

[C] The bundle of rights associated with ownership

[D] The geographic location of the land

Correct answer: [C] The bundle of rights associated with ownership.

Explanation: Real property includes not only the physical aspects of land and buildings (real estate) but also the rights of ownership, such as the right to use, sell, or lease the property. These legal rights are a key distinguishing factor that defines real property.

2. Which characteristic is unique to land and impacts its legal and economic value?

[A] Mobility

[B] Durability

[C] Uniqueness

[D] Flexibility

Correct answer: [C] Uniqueness.

Explanation: The uniqueness of each parcel of land, due to its fixed geographic location, directly impacts its value and is a fundamental characteristic that influences legal, economic, and development considerations in real estate.

Real Estate Market Dynamics

The real estate market is a complex and dynamic entity, influenced by a variety of factors that affect property values, market trends, and economic indicators. Understanding these influences is crucial for real estate professionals who aim to navigate the market effectively and make informed decisions for their clients. Key factors include economic conditions, interest rates, demographic shifts, and government policies, each playing a pivotal role in shaping the real estate landscape.

Economic conditions are a primary driver of the real estate market, with the overall health of the economy influencing buyer and seller behavior. In a strong economy, increased job security and higher income levels boost consumer confidence, leading to higher demand for real estate. Conversely, in a weaker economy, real estate demand may wane as consumers become more cautious with their spending. Interest rates also play a critical role, as lower rates make borrowing cheaper, potentially increasing the number of buyers in the market. Higher rates, however, can limit buying power, cooling the market.

Demographic shifts, such as changes in the age distribution of the population or migration patterns, can significantly impact real estate trends. For example, an aging population may increase demand for retirement homes, while urbanization trends can lead to higher demand for city dwellings. Government policies, including tax incentives, zoning laws, and housing regulations, further influence the real estate market by either encouraging or restricting development and investment in certain areas. Market trends, such as shifts towards sustainable and green living, also affect property values and buyer preferences. Properties that incorporate energy-efficient features or are located in areas with sustainable development practices may see an increase in value and demand. Additionally, technological advancements and the rise of smart homes are becoming increasingly important to modern buyers, influencing market trends and property values. Economic indicators relevant to real estate include housing starts, home sales figures, and price indices. Housing starts, or the number of new residential construction projects begun in a given period, can indicate the future supply of homes and potential market direction. Home sales figures, both new and existing, offer insights into market activity and trends. Price indices, such as the Case-Shiller Home Price Index, track changes in home prices over time, providing valuable information on market health and trends.

Exercise:

1. Which economic indicator is most directly related to the future supply of homes in the market?

[A] Interest rates

[B] Housing starts

[C] Home sales figures

[D] Price indices

Correct answer: [B] Housing starts.

Explanation: Housing starts refer to the commencement of new residential construction projects and are a direct indicator of the future supply of homes in the market. An increase in housing starts suggests a future increase in home supply, while a decrease indicates a potential tightening of the market.

2. How do demographic shifts influence the real estate market?

[A] By changing consumer preferences and demand for different types of properties

[B] By directly affecting interest rates and economic conditions

[C] By altering the legal framework surrounding real estate transactions

[D] By influencing the technological advancements in home construction

Correct answer: [A] By changing consumer preferences and demand for different types of properties.

Explanation: Demographic shifts, such as changes in population age or migration patterns, influence the real estate market by altering consumer preferences and demand for different types of properties, such as increased demand for retirement homes or urban apartments.

CHAPTER 3: UNDERSTANDING PROPERTY AND OWNERSHIP

Types of Property Ownership and Legal Rights

Property ownership in the United States is governed by a set of legal principles that define the rights and responsibilities of owners. Understanding these principles is crucial for real estate professionals who must navigate the complexities of property transactions. The primary types of property ownership include sole ownership, joint tenancy, tenancy in common, and community property, each with its own set of legal ramifications and rights.

Sole ownership, also known as tenancy in severalty, occurs when a property is owned by a single individual. This form of ownership grants the owner complete control over the property, including the right to sell, lease, or will the property to heirs. The legal simplicity of sole ownership makes it a straightforward arrangement, but it also places all financial and legal responsibilities on the individual owner. Joint tenancy is a form of co-ownership where two or more individuals hold property with rights of survivorship. This means that upon the death of one joint tenant, their interest in the property automatically passes to the surviving joint tenant(s), bypassing the probate process. Joint tenancy is characterized by four unities: unity of possession, interest, time, and title, meaning all joint tenants have equal rights to the entire property, acquire their interest at the same time, and through the same deed. Tenancy in common is another form of co-ownership, but unlike joint tenancy, there is no right of survivorship. Each tenant in common holds an individual, undivided interest in the property, which can be sold, leased, or transferred independently. Upon the death of a tenant in common, their interest passes to their heirs or as directed by their will, subject to probate. This type of ownership allows for unequal shares and the ability for each owner to dispose of their share independently.

Community property is a unique form of ownership based on the principle that property acquired during a marriage is owned jointly by both spouses. This concept is recognized in some states and applies to earnings, property bought with those earnings, and debts incurred during the marriage. Each spouse has equal management and control rights over community property, and upon the death of one spouse, their interest in the community property typically passes to the surviving spouse, unless otherwise directed by a will.

Exercise:

1. Which type of property ownership includes the right of survivorship?

[A] Sole ownership

[B] Joint tenancy

[C] Tenancy in common

[D] Community property

Correct answer: [B] Joint tenancy.

Explanation: Joint tenancy includes the right of survivorship, meaning that upon the death of one owner, their share of the property automatically passes to the surviving owner(s) without the need for probate.

2. In which type of property ownership can an owner's share be inherited by someone other than the co-owner?

[A] Sole ownership

[B] Joint tenancy

[C] Tenancy in common

[D] Community property

Correct answer: [C] Tenancy in common.

Explanation: Tenancy in common allows each owner to have an individual share of the property, which can be sold, leased, or transferred independently. Upon the death of a tenant in common, their share can be inherited by heirs or designated beneficiaries, not necessarily the co-owner.

3. Which form of property ownership is recognized only in some states and is based on the principle that property acquired during a marriage is owned jointly by both spouses?

[A] Sole ownership

[B] Joint tenancy

[C] Tenancy in common

[D] Community property

Correct answer: [D] Community property.

Explanation: Community property is a form of ownership recognized in some states, where property acquired during a marriage is considered jointly owned by both spouses, including property bought with earnings during the marriage and debts incurred during that time.

Property Types, Ownership, and Title Dynamics

The real estate landscape is diverse, encompassing a wide array of property types each with its own set of ownership and title characteristics. Residential properties, for instance, include single-family homes, condominiums, townhouses, and multifamily dwellings. These properties are primarily used for living purposes and their ownership can range from sole ownership, where a single individual holds the title, to joint tenancy or tenancy in common in cases such as condominiums where multiple parties may hold interest in a single property unit. Commercial properties, on the other hand, are utilized for business activities and include office buildings, retail spaces, warehouses, and shopping centers. Ownership of commercial properties often involves complex arrangements including partnerships, corporations, and real estate investment trusts (REITs), reflecting the significant investment and operational considerations associated with these assets. The title to commercial property may also be held in a leasehold interest, where a tenant has the right to use the property for a specified term under a lease agreement.

Industrial properties, characterized by their use for manufacturing, production, distribution, and storage, similarly can have varied ownership structures, often involving corporate entities or partnerships due to the large scale and specialized nature of these facilities. Titles to industrial properties must clearly delineate the extent of the property, including any easements for access or utilities, to avoid operational disruptions. Agricultural properties, including farms and ranches, present unique ownership considerations given their use of land for cultivation and livestock. Ownership may be in the form of sole proprietorships, partnerships, or corporations, with titles needing to accurately reflect boundaries and rights to water and mineral resources, which are critical to the property's value and use. Understanding the specifics of ownership and titles is crucial for real estate professionals, as each type of property and ownership structure presents distinct legal and financial implications. Titles must be clear and free of defects to ensure the transferability of the property. Title defects, such as liens, encumbrances, or disputes over property boundaries, can significantly impact a property transaction, leading to delays, financial losses, or litigation.

The process of transferring titles involves a thorough examination of the property's history to confirm the seller's right to transfer ownership and to identify any potential issues. This is typically conducted through a title search, followed by the issuance of title insurance to protect against unforeseen claims against the property.

Exercise:

1. Which type of property is primarily used for living purposes and can include ownership structures such as sole ownership and joint tenancy?

[A] Commercial

[B] Industrial

[C] Residential

[D] Agricultural

Correct answer: [C] Residential.

Explanation: Residential properties are designed for living purposes and can have various ownership structures, including sole ownership, where an individual owns the property outright, or joint tenancy, where two or more parties share ownership.

2. What is a leasehold interest most commonly associated with?

[A] Residential single-family homes

[B] Commercial properties

[C] Industrial land use

[D] Agricultural farms

Correct answer: [B] Commercial properties.

Explanation: A leasehold interest is typically associated with commercial properties, where a tenant has the right to use the property for business purposes under the terms of a lease agreement for a specified period.

3. Why is a title search important in the process of transferring property titles?

[A] To calculate property taxes

[B] To confirm the seller's right to transfer ownership and identify any title defects

[C] To determine the property's market value

[D] To inspect the property's condition

Correct answer: [B] To confirm the seller's right to transfer ownership and identify any title defects.

Explanation: A title search is conducted to ensure that the seller has the legal right to transfer the property and to uncover any issues such as liens, encumbrances, or disputes that could affect the sale and future ownership of the property.

Real vs. Personal Property: Definitions and Significance

Real property and personal property are two fundamental classifications in the realm of real estate that carry significant legal and financial implications. Real property, often referred to as real estate, encompasses land and any permanent structures attached to it, such as buildings or homes. This category is characterized by its immovable nature; once a structure is built on a piece of land, it typically remains there permanently. The legal rights associated with real property include the right to sell, lease, or use the land and its improvements, making it a critical component of real estate transactions.

Personal property, on the other hand, consists of movable items that are not permanently affixed to the land. This can include furniture, vehicles, electronics, and even intangible assets like stocks and bonds. The distinguishing factor between personal and real property lies in the item's mobility; personal property can be moved from one location to another, reflecting its temporary association with a particular piece of real estate. The distinction between real and personal property is not merely academic but has practical implications in real estate transactions and legal processes. For example, when purchasing a home, the buyer acquires the real property (the land and any structures on it) but may negotiate separately for personal property items like the seller's furniture or appliances. Similarly, in estate planning, the differentiation determines how assets are distributed, with real property often requiring more formal transfer processes compared to personal property. In legal disputes, the classification of an item as real or personal property can affect the outcome significantly. For instance, fixtures—items that were once personal property but have been so affixed to the land or a structure that they are considered part of the real property—can be a point of contention in property sales or lease agreements. Determining whether an item is a fixture involves considering the method of attachment, the item's adaptation to the property, and the parties' intention.

Understanding the nuances between real and personal property enhances a real estate professional's ability to advise clients, structure transactions, and navigate legal challenges. It underscores the importance of clear agreements and thorough property inspections to identify and correctly classify all items involved in a real estate deal.

Exercise:

1. Which of the following is considered real property?

[A] A mobile home temporarily situated on a lot

[B] A built-in dishwasher

[C] A standing mirror in the living room

[D] A potted plant in the garden

Correct answer: [B] A built-in dishwasher.

Explanation: A built-in dishwasher is considered real property because it is attached to the home's structure, making it a permanent fixture. Unlike movable personal property, fixtures like a built-in dishwasher are integrated into the property, transferring along with the sale of the real estate.

2. What determines if an item is a fixture and thus considered real property?

[A] The item's value

[B] The owner's personal attachment to the item

[C] The method of attachment and the intention to make the item a permanent part of the property

[D] The color and design of the item

Correct answer: [C] The method of attachment and the intention to make the item a permanent part of the property.

Explanation: The classification of an item as a fixture, and thus real property, depends on how the item is attached to the property and whether there was an intention for it to remain permanently. This includes considerations of how the item is adapted to the property and the agreement between the parties involved.

3. Why is the distinction between real and personal property significant in real estate transactions?

[A] It affects the taxation of property

[B] It determines the items included in the sale of a property

[C] It influences the property's aesthetic appeal

[D] It dictates the color scheme of the property

Correct answer: [B] It determines the items included in the sale of a property.

Explanation: The distinction between real and personal property is crucial in real estate transactions because it clarifies what is included in the sale. Real property includes the land and any permanent structures, while personal property consists of movable items. This differentiation ensures both parties have a clear understanding of what is being bought and sold, preventing disputes and misunderstandings.

Property Legal Descriptions: Methods Explored

Legal descriptions of property serve as the definitive means of identifying a parcel of land's boundaries and location, a necessity in real estate transactions to ensure clarity and precision. Three primary methods are utilized in the United States: metes and bounds, the rectangular survey system, and the lot and block system. Each method offers a unique approach to property description, suitable for different types of landscapes and property divisions. Metes and bounds, one of the oldest methods, relies on detailed descriptions of a property's boundaries. Using natural landmarks, such as trees or rivers, and artificial markers, like streets or stakes, this method describes the perimeter of a property in a sequence of directions and distances. It begins and ends at the same point, forming a complete loop. The precision of metes and bounds descriptions is critical, especially in areas with irregular or unique property shapes, but can be complex and difficult to interpret without professional surveying knowledge. The rectangular survey system, also known as the Public Land Survey System (PLSS), was developed to simplify land division in the vast, undeveloped territories of the United States. It divides land into a grid of rectangles using principal meridians (north-south lines) and base lines (east-west lines). This system creates townships, sections, and fractions of sections, providing a standardized method for describing land that is especially effective in rural and undeveloped areas. The PLSS is favored for its simplicity and uniformity, making it easier to locate and define parcels without the need for detailed natural or artificial landmarks. The lot and block system is commonly used in developed areas, such as cities and suburbs, where land is divided into lots within blocks, which are then situated within subdivisions or tracts. This method references a recorded plat map, which shows the division of land into lots and blocks, providing an easy-to-follow reference that simplifies the identification of individual parcels. The lot and block system is particularly useful in residential and commercial real estate, where parcels are frequently bought and sold.

Exercise:

1. Which legal description method is most suitable for rural, undeveloped land?

[A] Metes and bounds

[B] Rectangular survey system

[C] Lot and block system

[D] All of the above

Correct answer: [B] Rectangular survey system.

Explanation: The rectangular survey system, or PLSS, is designed for simplicity and uniformity, making it most suitable for rural, undeveloped land. Its grid-like structure facilitates the division and description of large tracts of land without the need for detailed natural landmarks.

2. What is the starting point for a metes and bounds description?

[A] The northeasternmost point of the property

[B] The highest point on the property

[C] A designated landmark or marker

[D] The point of beginning, which is the same as the point of ending

Correct answer: [D] The point of beginning, which is the same as the point of ending.

Explanation: In a metes and bounds description, the description starts and ends at the same point, known as the "point of beginning." This method loops around the property's boundaries, detailing directions and distances until it returns to the starting point.

3. How does the lot and block system simplify property identification?

[A] By using natural landmarks

[B] By dividing land into a grid of rectangles

[C] By referencing a recorded plat map showing divisions into lots and blocks

[D] By describing the perimeter of a property in sequence

Correct answer: [C] By referencing a recorded plat map showing divisions into lots and blocks.

Explanation: The lot and block system simplifies property identification by referencing a recorded plat map, which details the division of land into lots and blocks within subdivisions. This method is particularly efficient in developed areas, providing a straightforward way to identify and describe individual parcels.

CHAPTER 4: LAND USE AND REGULATION

Government Oversight in Land Use and Legislation

Government oversight of land plays a pivotal role in shaping the landscape of real estate development, with federal, state, and local governments each holding specific responsibilities and powers. At the federal level, agencies such as the Environmental Protection Agency (EPA) enforce regulations that protect the environment and public health, impacting land use by restricting development in protected areas and managing hazardous waste. Federal laws like the Clean Water Act and the Endangered Species Act also set constraints on land use to preserve natural resources and biodiversity, which can influence the feasibility and planning of real estate projects. State governments have their own set of regulations and zoning laws that further dictate the use of land. These laws can vary significantly from one state to another, affecting everything from land development to environmental protection. States play a crucial role in managing resources and implementing policies that balance growth with conservation. They also oversee the licensing of real estate professionals, ensuring that agents and brokers comply with both state-specific and federal regulations. Local governments, including cities and counties, have the most direct influence on land use through zoning ordinances and building codes. Zoning laws determine the types of buildings and activities that are permissible in different areas, segregating residential neighborhoods from commercial and industrial zones, and influencing the density of development. Building codes set standards for construction, safety, and accessibility, ensuring that structures are safe and habitable. Local planning commissions review development proposals to ensure compliance with these regulations, guiding the growth of communities in alignment with long-term plans and visions.

Key legislation that impacts land use decisions includes the Comprehensive Environmental Response, Compensation, and Liability Act (CERCLA), commonly known as Superfund, which addresses the cleanup of contaminated sites. The National Environmental Policy Act (NEPA) requires environmental assessments for projects with federal involvement, influencing land use by identifying potential environmental impacts and alternatives to proposed actions.

Understanding the interplay between government oversight and land use is crucial for real estate professionals, as it affects the valuation, development potential, and legal compliance of properties. Navigating these regulations requires a thorough understanding of the various layers of government policies and procedures that govern land use.

Exercise:

Which federal act requires environmental assessments for projects with federal involvement to identify potential environmental impacts?

[A] Clean Water Act

[B] Endangered Species Act

[C] National Environmental Policy Act (NEPA)

[D] Comprehensive Environmental Response, Compensation, and Liability Act (CERCLA)

Correct Answer: [C] National Environmental Policy Act (NEPA)

Explanation: The National Environmental Policy Act (NEPA) mandates environmental assessments for significant projects involving federal funding or permits to evaluate potential environmental impacts and explore alternative actions. This act plays a critical role in land use planning and decision-making, ensuring that environmental considerations are integrated into the federal decision-making process.

Building Codes: Safety, Compliance, and Impact on Development

Building codes and regulations serve as the backbone of construction safety and compliance, ensuring that structures not only meet minimum safety standards but also adhere to a set of guidelines that promote the well-being of occupants and the community at large. These codes cover a broad spectrum of considerations, from structural integrity to fire safety, and accessibility, each designed to address specific risks and requirements inherent in the construction and use of buildings. Fire codes are critical components of building regulations, focusing on minimizing the risk and spread of fires within structures. These codes dictate the use of fire-resistant materials, the installation of smoke detectors and sprinkler systems, and the design of safe evacuation routes. Compliance with fire codes not only protects lives but also significantly reduces the potential for property damage in the event of a fire.

Structural integrity regulations are designed to ensure that buildings can withstand typical loads and forces, including the weight of the building itself, occupants, and environmental stresses such as wind and seismic activity. These regulations dictate the quality of materials, construction practices, and engineering standards required to create safe, durable structures. Ensuring structural integrity is paramount, especially in areas prone to natural disasters, as it directly impacts the safety of the building's occupants and the resilience of the community. Accessibility standards, such as those outlined in the Americans with Disabilities Act (ADA), ensure that buildings are accessible to individuals with disabilities. These standards cover a wide range of design criteria, including wheelchair accessibility, the provision of Braille and tactile signs, and the design of accessible restrooms and public spaces. Compliance with accessibility standards not only fulfills a legal requirement but also promotes inclusivity, ensuring that all individuals, regardless of physical ability, can use and enjoy public and private spaces. The impact of these regulations on real estate development is profound. Developers must navigate these codes from the earliest stages of planning and design, through construction, to the final inspection and certification of buildings. Compliance with building codes and regulations not only ensures the safety and usability of structures but also affects the project's timeline, budget, and overall feasibility. Real estate professionals must be knowledgeable about these regulations, as they directly influence property values, marketability, and the legal responsibilities of property owners and developers.

Exercise:

What is the primary purpose of fire codes in building regulations?

[A] To ensure the aesthetic appeal of buildings

[B] To minimize the risk and spread of fires within structures

[C] To reduce construction costs

[D] To increase the resale value of properties

Correct Answer: [B] To minimize the risk and spread of fires within structures

Explanation: Fire codes are an essential part of building regulations, focusing specifically on measures that prevent the outbreak of fires and limit their spread within structures. These codes mandate the use of fire-resistant materials, the installation of fire detection and suppression systems, and the design of safe evacuation routes, all aimed at protecting lives and minimizing property damage in the event of a fire.

Land Use, Zoning, and Environmental Impact

Zoning laws serve as a critical tool for municipalities to control the physical development of land and the kinds of uses to which each individual property may be put. Zoning ordinances divide a city or county into different areas or "zones," restricting the types of buildings and activities that can take place in each area. Residential, commercial, industrial, and agricultural are common zoning categories, each with its own set of regulations concerning building heights, densities, and layout, as well as the specific types of activities permitted. Environmental regulations work in tandem with zoning laws to ensure that land use does not adversely affect the environment. These laws, enforced at federal, state, and local levels, aim to protect natural resources and ensure sustainable development. They cover a wide range of issues, including air and water quality, waste management, and the preservation of wildlife habitats. Environmental Impact Assessments (EIAs) are often required before the approval of large-scale development projects to identify potential negative environmental effects and propose mitigation strategies.

The interplay between zoning and environmental regulations significantly influences urban planning and development. Zoning laws help shape the physical layout of communities, determining where homes, businesses, and industrial activities are located. They can encourage the development of compact, walkable communities with mixed-use developments, or they can promote sprawling, car-dependent suburbs. Environmental regulations ensure that development is done sustainably, protecting water sources, preserving open spaces, and minimizing pollution. These regulations also have a profound impact on real estate values. Properties located in zones that permit a wide range of uses or in areas with fewer environmental restrictions generally command higher prices. Conversely, properties subject to stringent environmental protections or located in zones with limited permissible uses may see their development potential and market value limited.

Understanding zoning and environmental regulations is crucial for real estate professionals, as these laws can significantly affect property development potential, investment value, and the legal use of land.

Professionals must navigate these regulations when advising clients, planning developments, or evaluating investment opportunities.

Exercise:

What is the primary purpose of zoning laws?

[A] To increase tax revenue for municipalities

[B] To regulate land use and development

[C] To standardize building designs across cities

[D] To eliminate the need for environmental regulations

Correct Answer: [B] To regulate land use and development

Explanation: Zoning laws are enacted by municipalities to control the development of land and the types of uses that are permitted in different areas within a city or county. These laws help ensure that land use is organized and consistent with the community's long-term planning goals, such as promoting residential neighborhoods' safety, ensuring commercial areas are accessible, and preserving spaces for industrial activities. By dividing land into zones, such as residential, commercial, and industrial, zoning laws regulate building heights, densities, and the layout of developments, as well as the specific activities that are permitted in each zone, thereby shaping the physical and functional characteristics of communities.

Special Land Use Types and Regulations

Special categories of land use such as agricultural, recreational, and historical lands are governed by unique regulations and protections that significantly influence their ownership and development. Agricultural land use is primarily dedicated to farming activities, including cultivation of crops and raising livestock. This type of land is often protected by zoning laws that limit non-agricultural development to preserve farming areas and maintain food production capabilities. Recreational land use encompasses areas designated for leisure and entertainment purposes, such as parks, sports fields, and golf courses. These areas may benefit from specific zoning ordinances that protect open spaces and ensure public access. Historical lands include sites of historical or cultural significance, often protected by laws that restrict alterations and require preservation efforts to maintain their integrity for future generations. The implications of these regulations for ownership and development are profound. Owners of agricultural land may face restrictions on converting their property to residential or commercial uses, preserving the agricultural character of the area but potentially limiting its market value. Recreational land owners must balance public access with maintenance and safety concerns, often requiring significant investment to meet regulatory standards. Owners of historical lands bear the responsibility of preservation, which can include costly renovations and adherence to strict guidelines for any changes to the property.

For real estate professionals, understanding the specific regulations and protections associated with these special land use types is crucial when advising clients on purchasing, developing, or selling such properties. This knowledge ensures compliance with laws and maximizes the property's value and utility.

Exercise:

What is a primary consideration for owners of historical land?

[A] Maximizing the number of visitors to the site

[B] Converting the land to residential use

[C] Adhering to preservation guidelines and restrictions

[D] Developing the land for industrial purposes

Correct Answer: [C] Adhering to preservation guidelines and restrictions

Explanation: Owners of historical lands are primarily concerned with adhering to preservation guidelines and restrictions, which are in place to protect the historical or cultural significance of the property. These guidelines often dictate how renovations and changes to the property can be made, ensuring that its integrity and value as a historical site are maintained for future generations. This responsibility distinguishes historical land use from other types, where development may be more focused on economic gain or utility maximization.

Chapter 5: Valuation and Market Analysis

Basics of Property Valuation

Property valuation is a critical component in the real estate industry, serving as the cornerstone for buying, selling, financing, and investing decisions. At its core, property valuation involves estimating the value of a real estate property based on a set of predetermined factors and methodologies. Key factors influencing property value include location, condition, and market conditions, each playing a pivotal role in determining a property's worth in the current real estate market. Location is often cited as the most crucial factor in property valuation. The adage "location, location, location" underscores the significance of geographical placement, with properties in desirable areas commanding higher prices. Desirability can be influenced by various factors such as proximity to amenities, quality of local schools, employment opportunities, and overall neighborhood appeal. Additionally, location encompasses aspects like the safety of the area, accessibility to public transportation, and potential for future development, all of which can significantly impact property values. The condition of the property is another vital factor in valuation. A well-maintained property with modern features and updates typically has a higher value compared to a property in disrepair or needing significant updates. The property's age, architectural style, layout, and the quality of construction materials also contribute to its overall condition and, consequently, its valuation. Regular maintenance and upgrades can enhance a property's appeal to potential buyers, thereby increasing its market value. Market conditions play a dynamic role in property valuation, reflecting the current economic climate, interest rates, and the real estate market's supply and demand. Economic indicators such as employment rates, consumer confidence, and GDP growth can influence buyers' purchasing power and, thus, property values. Additionally, the real estate market operates on a cyclical basis, with periods of growth (a seller's market) and decline (a buyer's market), each affecting property values differently. Understanding these cycles and market trends is essential for accurate property valuation. Methodologies used in property valuation include the sales comparison approach, the cost approach, and the income approach. The sales comparison approach involves comparing the property with similar properties that have recently sold in the same area, adjusting for differences to arrive at a value. The cost approach estimates the cost to replace the property, considering depreciation, to determine its value. The income approach is used primarily for rental properties, calculating value based on the income the property generates.

Exercise:

Which factor is most crucial in determining a property's value?

[A] Color of the property

[B] Location

[C] Number of windows

[D] Style of the roof

Correct Answer: [B] Location

Explanation: Location is the most critical factor in determining a property's value due to its significant impact on desirability and demand. Properties in sought-after areas, with access to amenities, good schools, and employment opportunities, tend to have higher values compared to those in less desirable locations. This principle highlights the importance of geographical placement in the real estate market, influencing buyers' willingness to pay a premium for properties in prime locations.

Fundamentals of Real Estate Valuation

The theoretical principles underlying real estate valuation form the bedrock upon which practical valuation methodologies stand. These principles, deeply rooted in economic theory, guide the assessment of property values and provide a framework for understanding market dynamics. The principle of supply and demand is fundamental to real estate valuation, positing that the value of property is directly related to the balance between the quantity of real estate available and the desire of buyers to own it. When demand exceeds supply, prices tend to rise, whereas an excess of supply over demand leads to price decreases. This principle underscores the importance of market conditions in valuation efforts. The highest and best use principle asserts that the value of a property reaches its peak when the property is utilized in a way that is legally permissible, physically possible, financially feasible, and maximally productive. This concept encourages the examination of a property's potential uses and the selection of the one that adds the highest value. It is crucial for real estate professionals to consider not just the current use but also potential alternative uses that could increase the property's market value.

Substitution, another core principle, holds that the value of a property is influenced by the cost of acquiring an equally desirable alternative property. This principle drives the comparative market analysis approach, where properties are valued based on the prices of similar properties in the vicinity. It emphasizes the buyer's perspective, suggesting that a property's value is capped by the cost of acquiring a substitute that meets the buyer's needs and preferences. Conformity suggests that a property's value is maximized when it conforms to the standards of its surroundings. Properties that fit well within a neighborhood, matching in style, condition, and use, tend to have higher values than those that are significantly different. This principle highlights the importance of the property's context within its local environment and the impact of neighborhood characteristics on value. Anticipation reflects the impact of future benefits or detriments on a property's current value. Real estate investments are often made with an eye toward future income streams, appreciation, and potential changes in the market. This principle underscores the forward-looking nature of real estate valuation, where the expected future benefits are factored into the current valuation.

Exercise:

Which principle of real estate valuation suggests that a property's value is influenced by the cost of acquiring an equally desirable substitute?

[A] Supply and Demand

[B] Highest and Best Use

[C] Substitution

[D] Conformity

Correct Answer: [C] Substitution

Explanation: The principle of substitution underlies the concept that a property's value is determined by what it would cost to purchase an equally desirable alternative property. This principle is central to comparative market analysis, where the value of a property is assessed in relation to similar properties in the same area. It reflects the buyer's perspective, considering the availability of comparable options and their prices, which serve as a benchmark for determining the subject property's value.

Property Appraisal: Process and Methods

The process of market value and appraisal in real estate transactions is a critical component that ensures properties are bought and sold at fair market value. The appraisal process begins with the initial inspection of the property, where the appraiser evaluates the condition of the property, its features, and any improvements or deficiencies that may affect its value. This inspection is thorough, covering both the interior and exterior of the property, and noting details such as square footage, room count, and the condition of the structure and its systems. Following the inspection, the appraiser employs various methods to determine the property's value. The most common appraisal methods include the sales comparison approach, the cost approach, and the income approach. The sales comparison approach compares the subject property with similar properties that have recently sold in the same area, adjusting for differences to arrive at a value. The cost approach estimates the cost to replace the property's structures, minus depreciation, plus the land value. The income approach, used primarily for rental properties, calculates value based on the income the property generates, considering factors like rent levels, occupancy rates, and operating expenses.

The appraiser gathers and analyzes data from multiple sources, including local real estate listings, public property records, and recent sales data, to support the valuation. This analysis is compiled into a detailed appraisal report that includes the appraiser's findings, the methods used to determine value, and the final estimated market value of the property. The report also contains information about the property's location, comparisons with similar properties, and market trends that may influence value. The importance of objective valuation in real estate transactions cannot be overstated. An accurate appraisal ensures that buyers do not overpay for a property and that sellers receive a fair price. It also plays a crucial role in the mortgage lending process, as lenders require appraisals to confirm that the property's value supports the loan amount. Objective valuation protects all parties involved in the transaction, promoting transparency and fairness in the real estate market.

Exercise:

Which appraisal method estimates the property's value based on the income the property generates?

[A] Sales Comparison Approach

[B] Cost Approach

[C] Income Approach

[D] Replacement Value Method

Correct Answer: [C] Income Approach

Explanation: The income approach to property valuation calculates a property's value based on the income it generates, making it particularly suitable for rental properties and investment real estate. This method considers factors such as rent levels, occupancy rates, operating expenses, and the potential for future income, providing an estimate of value that reflects the property's ability to generate revenue. This approach is distinct from the sales comparison and cost approaches, which focus on recent sales of comparable properties and the cost to replace the property's structures, respectively.

Valuation Techniques Overview

Comparative and valuation techniques are essential tools for real estate professionals, enabling them to determine the value of properties with accuracy and confidence. Among these techniques, the Comparative Market Analysis (CMA) stands out as a fundamental approach. CMA involves evaluating similar properties that have recently sold, are currently on the market, or were listed but did not sell within a specific area. This analysis helps in establishing a price range for a property by comparing it to others with similar characteristics, such as location, size, and condition. The effectiveness of CMA hinges on the availability of comparable data and the professional's ability to adjust for differences between the subject property and the comparables, making it particularly useful in active markets where ample data exists.

The cost approach is another critical technique, primarily used when comparable sales data is scarce, such as with unique or specialized properties. This method calculates a property's value by adding the land value to the current cost of constructing a replica of the existing building, minus depreciation. It is based on the principle of substitution, which assumes that a rational buyer would not pay more for an existing property than the cost to build a similar property on a comparable piece of land. The cost approach is particularly relevant for new buildings or those with unique features that make finding comparable sales challenging. The income approach is vital for valuing investment and commercial properties. This method focuses on the income-generating potential of the property, converting future income streams into a present value. It involves determining the net operating income (NOI) of the property, which is the total income minus operating expenses, and then applying a capitalization rate (cap rate) to arrive at the property's value. The cap rate reflects the investor's required rate of return based on the perceived risk of the investment. This approach is best used for properties with stable income streams, such as apartment buildings, office spaces, and retail locations.

The sales comparison approach is closely related to CMA but is more formalized and typically used in appraisals. This method directly compares the subject property with similar properties that have recently sold, adjusting for any differences to determine the value. Adjustments may be made for factors such as location, size, condition, and features. The sales comparison approach is widely regarded as the most indicative of market value, provided there are sufficient recent comparables to establish a reliable comparison.

Exercise:

Which valuation technique is primarily used for investment and commercial properties to determine value based on income-generating potential?

[A] Comparative Market Analysis

[B] Cost Approach

[C] Income Approach

[D] Sales Comparison Approach

Correct Answer: [C] Income Approach

Explanation: The income approach is specifically designed to value investment and commercial properties by focusing on their ability to generate income. This method calculates the property's value based on the net operating income it produces, adjusted by a capitalization rate that reflects the investor's required rate of return. This approach is particularly useful for properties with stable and predictable income streams, making it the preferred method for evaluating commercial real estate investments.

Analyzing Real Estate Market Dynamics

Analyzing market trends, demand, and supply in the real estate sector involves a multifaceted approach, focusing on economic conditions, interest rates, and demographic shifts. Economic conditions play a pivotal role, as they directly impact people's ability to purchase homes. A strong economy, characterized by low unemployment and rising incomes, typically fosters higher demand for real estate, pushing prices upward. Conversely, during economic downturns, demand may wane, leading to a potential decrease in property values. Interest rates are another critical factor; lower rates make borrowing cheaper, thereby increasing the affordability of real estate for buyers. This can lead to heightened demand and, subsequently, higher prices. On the other hand, when interest rates rise, borrowing costs increase, potentially dampening demand. Demographic shifts, such as changes in the age distribution of the population or migration patterns, also significantly influence real estate demand and supply. For instance, an aging population may increase the demand for smaller, more manageable properties or retirement communities. Similarly, regions experiencing an influx of residents may see heightened demand for housing, driving up property values. Conversely, areas suffering from population decline may witness a surplus of supply, leading to lower prices.

Understanding these dynamics requires real estate professionals to stay informed about current economic indicators, interest rate trends, and demographic data. This knowledge enables them to anticipate market shifts and advise clients accordingly, whether they are buyers, sellers, or investors.

Exercise:

Which factor is most likely to increase the demand for smaller, more manageable properties?

[A] A decrease in interest rates

[B] An economic downturn

[C] An aging population

[D] A decrease in the unemployment rate

Correct Answer: [C] An aging population

Explanation: An aging population is more likely to seek smaller, more manageable properties that meet their needs for comfort and accessibility without the maintenance demands of larger homes. This demographic shift can significantly influence real estate demand patterns, contrasting with the effects of changes in interest rates, economic conditions, or employment trends, which have broader impacts on the market's overall demand and supply dynamics.

Market Analysis for Real Estate Decisions

Conducting a comprehensive market analysis (CMA) is a critical process for real estate professionals aiming to make informed decisions and price properties accurately. This analysis involves a detailed examination of the real estate market in a specific area, focusing on properties similar to the one being sold or purchased. The goal is to determine a fair market value by comparing the subject property to recently sold properties with similar characteristics. Key steps in conducting a CMA include identifying comparable properties (comps), adjusting for differences between the comps and the subject property, and analyzing the outcomes to set a competitive market price. Identifying comps requires access to current and reliable real estate data, including recent sales, listings, and expired listings. Real estate professionals use this data to select properties that are most similar to the subject property in terms of location, size, condition, and features. It's important to consider properties sold within the last three to six months to ensure the analysis reflects the current market conditions.

Adjusting for differences is a nuanced process where the real estate professional adds or subtracts value from the comps based on features that differ from the subject property. For example, if a comp has one more bedroom than the subject property, the value of that extra bedroom is subtracted from the comp's sale price. This adjustment process ensures a like-for-like comparison between the subject property and the comps. Analyzing the outcomes involves synthesizing the adjusted sale prices of the comps to arrive at a suggested market value for the subject property. This suggested value is a starting point for pricing the property and may be adjusted based on the real estate professional's expertise and understanding of the market dynamics.

A comprehensive market analysis goes beyond a CMA by incorporating broader market trends, economic indicators, and supply and demand dynamics. This analysis looks at how external factors such as interest rates, economic growth, and demographic shifts impact the real estate market in the area of interest. By understanding these broader trends, real estate professionals can provide strategic advice to clients, whether they are looking to buy, sell, or invest.

Exercise:

What is the primary purpose of adjusting for differences between the subject property and the comps in a Comparative Market Analysis (CMA)?

[A] To reflect the current market conditions more accurately

[B] To ensure a like-for-like comparison between properties

[C] To determine the economic growth in the area

[D] To analyze broader market trends

Correct Answer: [B] To ensure a like-for-like comparison between properties

Explanation: Adjusting for differences between the subject property and the comps is essential to ensure a like-for-like comparison. This process involves adding or subtracting value based on features that differ from the subject property, such as the number of bedrooms, property size, and location nuances. By making these adjustments, real estate professionals can accurately compare the subject property to similar properties that have recently sold, leading to a fair and competitive market price determination.

CHAPTER 6: REAL ESTATE FINANCING

Fundamentals of Real Estate Finance

Real estate finance plays a pivotal role in the purchase and sale of properties, acting as the backbone of the real estate market by providing the necessary capital for buyers to secure their investments. Understanding the basics of real estate finance is crucial for any aspiring real estate professional, as it encompasses the methods through which properties are funded, the types of loans available, and the terms and conditions that govern these financial transactions. Financing in real estate purchases involves a variety of loans, each with its specific terms, conditions, and eligibility criteria, tailored to meet the diverse needs of borrowers. At the core of real estate finance is the mortgage loan, a type of loan specifically designed for the purchase of real property. Mortgages are secured loans, meaning the property itself serves as collateral for the loan. If the borrower fails to repay the loan according to the agreed terms, the lender has the right to foreclose on the property to recover the outstanding debt. The terms of a mortgage loan, including the interest rate, repayment period, and down payment, significantly influence the overall cost of purchasing a property and the monthly financial obligations of the borrower. Interest rates on mortgage loans can be either fixed or adjustable. A fixed-rate mortgage locks in the interest rate for the duration of the loan, providing stability and predictability in monthly payments. Conversely, an adjustable-rate mortgage (ARM) has an interest rate that can change periodically based on fluctuations in the broader financial market, which can lead to variations in monthly payments.

The down payment is another critical component of real estate financing, representing the buyer's initial equity in the property. Traditional lenders typically require a down payment of 20% of the property's purchase price, although there are programs available that allow for lower down payments, especially for first-time homebuyers or those who qualify for government-backed loans, such as FHA loans, which are insured by the Federal Housing Administration.

The repayment period, or loan term, usually spans from 15 to 30 years for most residential mortgages, affecting both the monthly payment amount and the total interest paid over the life of the loan. Shorter loan terms generally result in higher monthly payments but lower total interest costs, while longer terms spread out the repayment, resulting in lower monthly payments but higher total interest costs. Understanding these foundational concepts of real estate finance is essential for navigating the complexities of the real estate market and advising clients on the most suitable financing options for their needs. Real estate professionals must be well-versed in the various financing mechanisms available, as well as the implications of different loan terms and conditions, to effectively support their clients throughout the buying process.

Exercise:

What does a fixed-rate mortgage offer to borrowers?

[A] A variable interest rate that changes with market conditions

[B] An interest rate that remains the same throughout the life of the loan

[C] A lower interest rate in the initial years of the loan

[D] An interest rate that increases over time

Correct Answer: [B] An interest rate that remains the same throughout the life of the loan

Explanation: A fixed-rate mortgage provides stability and predictability to borrowers by maintaining the same interest rate for the entire duration of the loan. This means that the monthly mortgage payments remain constant, unaffected by fluctuations in the financial market, which can be particularly advantageous for long-term financial planning and budgeting.

Foundations of Real Estate Finance

Leverage, risk, security, and interest form the bedrock of real estate finance, each playing a pivotal role in the structuring and understanding of financial transactions within the real estate sector. Leverage, in the context of real estate, refers to the use of borrowed capital to increase the potential return of an investment. It allows investors to purchase properties they otherwise could not afford with cash alone, amplifying both potential gains and losses. The principle of risk is inherently tied to leverage; as leverage increases, so too does the risk associated with the investment. This risk is multifaceted, encompassing interest rate fluctuations, market volatility, and the potential for loss of income or principal. Security, another fundamental principle, pertains to the collateralization of real estate loans. In mortgage financing, the property itself serves as security for the loan. This means that if the borrower defaults on the loan, the lender has the right to seize the property to recoup the outstanding debt, a process known as foreclosure. The principle of interest is equally critical, representing the cost of borrowing money. Interest rates on mortgages can significantly affect the affordability of a loan and the overall cost of purchasing a property. They are determined by a variety of factors, including the lender's assessment of the borrower's creditworthiness, market conditions, and the Federal Reserve's monetary policy.

These principles are not isolated; they interact in complex ways that influence financing decisions and the real estate market at large. For instance, a low-interest-rate environment may encourage borrowing by reducing the cost of loans, thereby increasing demand for real estate and potentially driving up property prices. Conversely, high interest rates can lead to decreased demand and lower prices. Understanding these dynamics is crucial for real estate professionals, who must navigate the intricacies of financing options to advise their clients effectively.

Exercise:

What principle of real estate finance involves using borrowed capital to increase the potential return of an investment?

[A] Risk

[B] Security

[C] Leverage

[D] Interest

Correct Answer: [C] Leverage

Explanation: Leverage is the principle of using borrowed capital to finance the purchase of an asset, in this case, real estate, with the aim of increasing the potential return on investment. It allows investors to amplify their purchasing power, but also increases the risk of loss, as the potential for both gains and losses is magnified.

Real Estate Loans and Mortgages Explained

The real estate market offers a variety of loans and mortgages designed to meet the diverse financial needs and situations of buyers. Each type of loan has specific terms, conditions, and eligibility requirements, making some loans more suitable for certain buyers than others. Understanding these options is crucial for real estate professionals to guide their clients through the financing process effectively. Fixed-rate mortgages are one of the most common types of loans, offering a stable interest rate and monthly payment for the life of the loan, typically 15 to 30 years. This stability makes fixed-rate mortgages a popular choice for buyers who plan to stay in their homes for a long period and prefer predictable financial planning. Adjustable-rate mortgages (ARMs), on the other hand, begin with a fixed interest rate for a set initial term, after which the rate adjusts at predetermined intervals based on a specified financial index. ARMs can be suitable for buyers expecting to move or refinance before the initial fixed period ends, potentially benefiting from lower initial interest rates compared to fixed-rate mortgages. FHA loans, insured by the Federal Housing Administration, are designed to help first-time homebuyers and those with lower credit scores or smaller down payments. FHA loans require a minimum down payment as low as 3.5% and are more forgiving of lower credit scores, making homeownership more accessible to a broader range of buyers. VA loans, guaranteed by the Department of Veterans Affairs, offer significant benefits to eligible veterans, active-duty service members, and some surviving spouses. These loans require no down payment and do not necessitate private mortgage insurance (PMI), reducing the upfront and monthly costs for borrowers. VA loans also provide more flexible credit requirements, making them an invaluable resource for eligible military borrowers.

Each of these loan types serves different buyer needs and financial situations, emphasizing the importance of a comprehensive understanding of the options available. Real estate professionals must be equipped to advise clients on choosing the most appropriate mortgage based on their long-term goals, financial health, and eligibility for specific loan programs.

Exercise:

Which loan type is best suited for a buyer with a small down payment and lower credit score?

[A] Fixed-rate mortgage

[B] Adjustable-rate mortgage (ARM)

[C] FHA loan

[D] VA loan

Correct Answer: [C] FHA loan

Explanation: FHA loans are specifically designed to accommodate buyers with smaller down payments and lower credit scores. With the requirement of a minimum down payment as low as 3.5% and more lenient credit score requirements, FHA loans make homeownership more accessible to a wider range of buyers, particularly those who may not qualify for conventional loan products. This contrasts with fixed-rate and adjustable-rate mortgages, which typically have stricter credit score and down payment requirements, and VA loans, which are reserved for eligible veterans, active-duty service members, and certain surviving spouses.

Navigating the Mortgage Market and Loan Process

The mortgage market is a complex ecosystem, featuring a variety of key players, including lenders, brokers, and government agencies, each playing a pivotal role in the process of securing a mortgage. Lenders, typically banks or credit unions, provide the capital for the mortgage, whereas brokers act as intermediaries, helping borrowers find the best mortgage product to suit their needs. Government agencies like the Federal Housing Administration (FHA) and the Department of Veterans Affairs (VA) offer specific loan programs to eligible borrowers, often with advantageous terms. The process of securing a mortgage begins with the application, where the borrower provides financial information, including income, assets, debts, and credit history, to the lender. This information is crucial for the lender to assess the borrower's creditworthiness and determine the loan amount, interest rate, and terms they are willing to offer. The pre-approval stage follows, giving borrowers an estimate of how much they can afford, which is invaluable during the house hunting process. Once a property is selected and an offer is made, the loan application moves into the underwriting phase. During underwriting, the lender verifies the borrower's financial information, assesses the property's value through an appraisal, and evaluates the risk of lending. This phase is critical, as it determines whether the loan is approved. Upon loan approval, the closing process begins, involving the preparation and signing of various legal documents to finalize the loan and transfer the property ownership. This stage also includes the payment of closing costs, which are fees associated with finalizing the mortgage, such as loan origination fees, appraisal fees, and title insurance. The mortgage market and loan process are governed by various federal and state laws and regulations, designed to protect both borrowers and lenders. These regulations ensure transparency, fairness, and integrity in the lending process, requiring disclosures about loan terms, rights to rescind, and procedures for resolving disputes. Understanding the structure of the mortgage market and the step-by-step process of securing a mortgage is essential for real estate professionals. This knowledge enables them to guide their clients through the complexities of financing a home purchase, from initial application to closing.

Exercise:

What is the primary purpose of the underwriting phase in the mortgage loan process?

[A] To assess the property's value

[B] To verify the borrower's financial information and assess lending risk

[C] To prepare and sign the legal documents for property transfer

[D] To provide borrowers with an estimate of how much they can afford

Correct Answer: [B] To verify the borrower's financial information and assess lending risk

Explanation: The underwriting phase is crucial in the mortgage loan process as it involves verifying the borrower's financial information provided during the application stage and assessing the risk associated with lending to the borrower. This phase ensures that the borrower meets the lender's criteria for creditworthiness and that the loan amount does not exceed the value of the property being purchased, safeguarding both the lender's and borrower's interests.

Understanding Mortgage Interest Calculation

Calculating mortgage interest is a fundamental aspect of understanding real estate financing, directly impacting the total cost of a loan and the monthly payments a borrower is required to make. Mortgage interest can be calculated using either simple or compound interest methods, though most mortgages in the United States utilize simple interest calculated on a monthly basis. Simple interest is determined based on the principal balance of the loan, the interest rate, and the number of payment periods. The formula for calculating simple interest on a mortgage is Interest = Principal x Rate x Time, where Time is the payment period in years. This method results in a fixed monthly payment for the duration of the loan, assuming a fixed-rate mortgage. Compound interest, while less common in mortgage calculations, involves charging interest on both the principal amount and any accumulated interest from previous periods. This method can lead to higher overall interest costs over the life of the loan, as interest accumulates on top of interest. However, most residential mortgages are structured to avoid compound interest, focusing instead on a simple interest calculation to maintain consistent monthly payments. Interest rates play a crucial role in determining the monthly payment and overall interest paid over the life of the mortgage. A lower interest rate results in lower monthly payments and less interest paid over time, making the loan more affordable. Conversely, a higher interest rate increases the monthly payment and the total amount of interest paid. Understanding how interest rates affect mortgage payments is crucial for real estate professionals advising clients on loan options. Adjustable-rate mortgages (ARMs) introduce variability in interest rates and, consequently, monthly payments. ARMs typically start with a lower interest rate than fixed-rate mortgages, but the rate can change at specified times, affecting the amount of interest due and the monthly payment amount. Borrowers considering an ARM must understand how future rate adjustments can impact their payments and overall loan cost.

Exercise:

What is the result of a lower interest rate on a mortgage loan?

[A] Higher total interest paid over the life of the loan

[B] Lower monthly payments and less interest paid over time

[C] No impact on the monthly payments

[D] Increased variability in monthly payments

Correct Answer: [B] Lower monthly payments and less interest paid over time

Explanation: A lower interest rate on a mortgage loan directly results in lower monthly payments, as the amount of interest due each period is reduced. This also leads to less interest paid over the life of the loan, making the loan more affordable for the borrower. Lower interest rates can significantly impact the overall cost of borrowing, highlighting the importance of securing the best possible rate at the time of loan origination.

Mortgage Approval Essentials

The mortgage approval process is a critical step in purchasing real estate, requiring a thorough understanding of key financial concepts and criteria. Lenders assess various factors to determine a borrower's eligibility for a loan, including credit scores, debt-to-income (DTI) ratios, and loan-to-value (LTV) ratios. Each of these components plays a vital role in the lender's decision-making process. Credit scores are numerical representations of a borrower's creditworthiness, derived from credit reports and history. They reflect the borrower's ability to repay debts and are crucial in the mortgage approval process. Lenders typically require a minimum credit score to qualify for a mortgage, with higher scores often resulting in more favorable loan terms and interest rates. The exact score needed can vary by lender and loan type, but a score of 620 or higher is commonly required for conventional loans. Debt-to-income ratios are another critical factor considered by lenders. This ratio compares a borrower's monthly debt obligations to their gross monthly income, expressed as a percentage. It helps lenders evaluate a borrower's ability to manage monthly payments and repay the loan. Generally, lenders prefer a DTI ratio of 43% or lower, though some loan programs may allow higher ratios. Loan-to-value ratios measure the loan amount against the value of the property being purchased, indicating the equity or down payment the borrower has in the property. A lower LTV ratio is favorable as it suggests the borrower has more equity in the property, reducing the lender's risk. Most lenders require an LTV ratio of 80% or lower to avoid the need for private mortgage insurance (PMI), though specific requirements can vary. The mortgage approval process typically begins with a borrower submitting a loan application, including financial documentation such as income verification, asset statements, and credit reports. The lender then evaluates this information against their lending criteria to make a decision. If approved, the borrower will receive a loan offer detailing the terms, including the interest rate, loan amount, and repayment period.

Exercise:

What factor do lenders consider to determine a borrower's eligibility for a mortgage loan?

[A] Educational background

[B] Credit scores

[C] Employment history length

[D] Marital status

Correct Answer: [B] Credit scores

Explanation: Lenders consider credit scores as a primary factor in determining a borrower's eligibility for a mortgage loan. Credit scores provide lenders with a numerical summary of the borrower's creditworthiness, based on their credit history and current credit behavior. This score influences not only the approval decision but also the terms of the loan, including the interest rate. Other factors such as educational background, employment history length, and marital status may influence a borrower's financial situation but are not direct criteria for mortgage loan eligibility.

Navigating Mortgages and Foreclosures

Managing different mortgage types requires a nuanced understanding of each option's benefits and risks, as well as the strategies for handling potential financial difficulties that may lead to foreclosure. Borrowers must navigate the complexities of fixed-rate mortgages, adjustable-rate mortgages (ARMs), FHA loans, and VA loans, each offering distinct terms, interest rates, and repayment structures. Fixed-rate mortgages provide stability with consistent monthly payments, making financial planning more predictable. In contrast, ARMs offer lower initial rates that can adjust over time, potentially leading to higher future payments. FHA loans cater to those with lower credit scores or smaller down payments, while VA loans offer significant benefits to eligible veterans and service members, including no down payment requirements. Foreclosure, the legal process by which a lender attempts to recover the balance of a loan from a borrower who has stopped making payments, represents a significant risk associated with mortgage financing. To manage this risk, borrowers should proactively communicate with lenders at the first sign of financial distress. Many lenders prefer to avoid foreclosure due to its high cost and lengthy process, making them open to alternatives such as loan modifications, refinancing, or short sales. Loan modifications can adjust the terms of the original loan to lower the monthly payment, while refinancing may provide a lower interest rate or extend the loan term. A short sale allows the borrower to sell the property for less than the outstanding mortgage balance, with the lender's approval, as a means to avoid foreclosure. Lenders play a crucial role in managing foreclosures, often having dedicated departments to work with borrowers facing financial difficulties. They assess the borrower's financial situation, the property's value, and market conditions to determine the most viable solution. Foreclosure alternatives not only help borrowers avoid the negative impacts on their credit scores and financial history but also allow lenders to mitigate losses.

Exercise:

What is a viable strategy for a borrower facing financial difficulties to avoid foreclosure?

[A] Ceasing all communications with the lender

[B] Waiting for the lender to initiate foreclosure proceedings

[C] Applying for a loan modification or refinancing

[D] Immediately filing for bankruptcy

Correct Answer: [C] Applying for a loan modification or refinancing

Explanation: Applying for a loan modification or refinancing is a proactive strategy for borrowers facing financial difficulties to avoid foreclosure. These options can provide more manageable loan terms, such as lower interest rates or extended repayment periods, thereby reducing monthly payments and making it easier for the borrower to meet their financial obligations. Ceasing communication with the lender, waiting for foreclosure proceedings to begin, or immediately filing for bankruptcy do not address the underlying issue of making the mortgage more affordable and can lead to more severe financial consequences.

Credit Law in Real Estate Financing

The Fair Credit Reporting Act (FCRA) and the Equal Credit Opportunity Act (ECOA) are pivotal in real estate financing, ensuring fair treatment and compliance in lending practices. The FCRA governs the collection, dissemination, and use of consumer information, including credit information used by lenders to make decisions on mortgage applications. It mandates that consumer reporting agencies maintain accurate and complete information to prevent misinformation from adversely affecting credit decisions. Under the FCRA, consumers have the right to view their credit reports, dispute inaccuracies, and receive notifications if information in their credit report has been used against them in a lending decision.

The ECOA prohibits discrimination in any aspect of a credit transaction based on race, color, religion, national origin, sex, marital status, age, or because all or part of an applicant's income derives from any public assistance program. This ensures that all consumers are given an equal opportunity to obtain credit, including mortgages for real estate. Lenders must provide applicants with explanations if their credit applications are denied, offering transparency in the decision-making process and an opportunity for applicants to address any discrepancies or misunderstandings. Both laws play a crucial role in real estate financing by promoting accuracy, fairness, and equal opportunity in the credit evaluation process. They protect consumers from unfair credit practices and discrimination while providing a framework for lenders to follow, ensuring that credit decisions are based on relevant, accurate information.

Exercise:

Which law requires lenders to provide explanations for denied credit applications?

[A] Fair Credit Reporting Act (FCRA)

[B] Equal Credit Opportunity Act (ECOA)

[C] Truth in Lending Act (TILA)

[D] Real Estate Settlement Procedures Act (RESPA)

Correct Answer: [B] Equal Credit Opportunity Act (ECOA)

Explanation: The Equal Credit Opportunity Act (ECOA) mandates that lenders must provide applicants with explanations if their credit applications are denied. This requirement is part of the ECOA's broader aim to prevent discrimination in the credit industry and ensure that all applicants are treated fairly and equally, regardless of personal characteristics unrelated to their creditworthiness. This contrasts with the FCRA, which focuses on the accuracy and privacy of credit reporting, and TILA and RESPA, which deal with disclosures and procedures in lending and real estate transactions, respectively.

CHAPTER 7: REAL ESTATE AGENCY BASICS

Real Estate Agency Types and Agent Duties

In the realm of real estate, understanding the nuances of agency relationships is crucial for both agents and clients to ensure successful transactions. Agency relationships in real estate are governed by state laws and can significantly influence the buying and selling process. These relationships are established through agreements between a client and an agent, detailing the agent's authority to act on the client's behalf in real estate transactions. The most common types of agency relationships include exclusive right to sell, exclusive agency, and open agency. Exclusive right to sell agreements grant one agent the exclusive right to sell a property, ensuring they receive a commission regardless of who finds the buyer. This type of agreement incentivizes the agent to invest maximum effort into marketing the property and securing the best possible deal for their client. Exclusive agency agreements, on the other hand, allow the property owner to sell the property independently without paying a commission to the agent. However, if the agent is the one who brings in the buyer, they are entitled to a commission. Open agency agreements permit the owner to engage multiple agents to find a buyer for the property, with only the agent who successfully secures a buyer entitled to a commission. This scenario fosters competition among agents but may result in less dedicated effort per agent. The responsibilities and duties of real estate agents under these agreements are defined by their fiduciary duties, which are paramount to the agent-client relationship. These duties include loyalty, where the agent must act in the best interest of their client above all others, including their own interests. Confidentiality is another critical duty, requiring agents to safeguard their clients' private information during and after the transaction process. Agents are also obligated to provide full disclosure, offering all relevant information about the property and transaction to their client. Moreover, agents must exercise reasonable care and diligence, ensuring they perform their duties to the best of their abilities and knowledge. Lastly, agents are required to account for all funds and properties related to the transaction, maintaining transparency and trust.

Exercise:

Which type of agency agreement requires the agent to be paid a commission regardless of who finds the buyer?

[A] Exclusive right to sell

[B] Exclusive agency

[C] Open agency

[D] None of the above

Correct Answer: [A] Exclusive right to sell

Explanation: The exclusive right to sell agreement uniquely positions the agent to receive a commission no matter who ultimately finds the buyer, whether it's the agent, the seller, or another party. This arrangement ensures that the agent is compensated for their efforts in marketing and selling the property, providing a strong incentive to secure the best possible deal for their client. Unlike exclusive agency or open agency agreements, where the agent's commission is contingent upon their direct involvement in finding the buyer, the exclusive right to sell offers the agent a guaranteed commission, aligning their interests closely with those of the seller.

Agency and Agent Types in Real Estate

Agency relationships in real estate are foundational to understanding how transactions are facilitated and the roles individuals play within these transactions. At the core of these relationships are the principal, agent, and third party. The principal is the individual who grants authority to another, the agent, to act on their behalf in dealings with a third party. This third party is typically someone looking to enter into a transaction with the principal, such as a buyer in the case of a seller's agent.

Different types of agents serve in real estate transactions, each with specific roles and responsibilities. Listing agents, also known as seller's agents, represent the seller in a real estate transaction. Their primary duties include marketing the property, advising the seller on offers, and assisting in the negotiation process to achieve the best possible sale terms for the seller. Buyer's agents, on the other hand, represent the buyer, providing guidance on property selection, negotiating purchase terms, and helping navigate the buying process. Dual agents represent both the buyer and the seller in the same transaction. While dual agency can streamline communication and transactions, it also requires careful management to ensure the agent impartially represents both parties' interests without conflict. The distinctions between these agent types are critical for real estate professionals to understand, as they dictate the nature of the fiduciary duties owed and the level of service provided to clients. Fiduciary duties include loyalty, confidentiality, disclosure, obedience, accounting, and reasonable care, which are paramount in ensuring the agent acts in the best interest of their client.

Exercise:

Which type of real estate agent represents both the buyer and the seller in the same transaction?

[A] Listing agent

[B] Buyer's agent

[C] Dual agent

[D] Independent agent

Correct Answer: [C] Dual agent

Explanation: A dual agent represents both the buyer and the seller in a single real estate transaction. This role requires the agent to balance the interests of both parties without favoring one over the other, ensuring fair and impartial representation. Dual agency can offer efficiencies in communication and negotiation but must be managed with a clear understanding of the responsibilities and limitations involved to prevent conflicts of interest.

Ethics and Legalities in Real Estate

Ethical and legal standards form the backbone of the real estate profession, ensuring that practitioners conduct their business with integrity, professionalism, and in compliance with both federal and state laws. The National Association of Realtors (NAR) Code of Ethics is a pivotal document that outlines the duties of real estate professionals to their clients, the public, and other realtors. It emphasizes honesty, fairness, and confidentiality, mandating that realtors put their clients' interests above their own and treat all parties to a transaction honestly. The Code is divided into three main areas: Duties to Clients and Customers, Duties to the Public, and Duties to Realtors, each encompassing specific standards of practice that guide realtors in their daily operations. State-specific legal requirements complement the NAR Code of Ethics, addressing issues such as licensing, continuing education, and specific disclosures that must be made in real estate transactions. These laws vary from state to state but generally aim to protect consumers by ensuring that real estate professionals are qualified, knowledgeable, and adhere to high ethical standards. For instance, many states require agents to disclose any personal interest they have in a property, whether they are representing a family member in a transaction, or if they are operating under a dual agency arrangement. Real estate professionals must navigate a complex landscape of legal obligations, from understanding the intricacies of contract law to complying with fair housing regulations. Fair housing laws, for example, prohibit discrimination in the sale, rental, and financing of dwellings based on race, color, national origin, religion, sex, familial status, or disability. Real estate agents must ensure that their marketing practices, property listings, and client interactions comply with these laws to avoid legal repercussions and uphold the ethical standards of their profession.

Exercise:

What is the primary purpose of the National Association of Realtors (NAR) Code of Ethics?

[A] To regulate the financial aspects of real estate transactions

[B] To outline the professional duties of realtors to clients, the public, and other realtors

[C] To provide a legal framework for real estate licensing and education

[D] To enforce state-specific real estate laws

Correct Answer: [B] To outline the professional duties of realtors to clients, the public, and other realtors

Explanation: The NAR Code of Ethics primarily serves to establish the professional duties and ethical standards that realtors must adhere to in their interactions with clients, the public, and fellow realtors. It emphasizes principles such as honesty, fairness, and confidentiality, aiming to foster trust in the real estate profession and ensure that realtors conduct their business in a manner that protects and serves the best interests of their clients and the public. This distinguishes the Code from legal frameworks and financial regulations, focusing instead on ethical conduct and professional integrity within the real estate industry.

Forming and Ending Agency Relationships

Agency relationships in real estate are pivotal, forming the basis of interaction between agents and their clients. These relationships are initiated through mutual consent, typically formalized in a written agreement that outlines the scope of the agent's authority and responsibilities. The formation of an agency relationship requires clear communication and agreement on terms, ensuring both parties understand their roles and obligations. This agreement, often referred to as a listing agreement in the context of sales or a management agreement for property management, specifies the duration of the relationship, compensation, and the specific duties the agent is authorized to perform on behalf of the principal. Termination of agency relationships can occur for several reasons, including the natural expiration of the agreement, fulfillment of the agency's purpose (such as the sale of a property), mutual agreement to end the relationship, or revocation by the principal. However, termination must adhere to any conditions specified in the original agreement to avoid legal complications. For instance, a principal cannot arbitrarily revoke an agent's authority without just cause if the agreement stipulates a fixed duration and conditions for termination. Similarly, an agent must provide proper notice and may have to fulfill certain obligations before ending the relationship, such as accounting for all funds and confidential information obtained during the tenure of the agreement. Upon termination, both parties have specific duties to ensure a smooth transition. The agent must return all documents, funds, and property related to the agency to the principal. Additionally, the agent must cease acting on behalf of the principal and inform any third parties of the termination to prevent unauthorized transactions. The principal, on the other hand, must fulfill any agreed-upon compensation or reimbursement for expenses incurred by the agent in the course of their duties.

Exercise:

What must an agent do upon the termination of an agency relationship?

[A] Continue to represent the principal until a replacement is found

[B] Return all documents, funds, and property related to the agency to the principal

[C] Immediately start representing a competing principal in the same transaction

[D] Retain all confidential information for potential future use

Correct Answer: [B] Return all documents, funds, and property related to the agency to the principal

Explanation: Upon the termination of an agency relationship, the agent is obligated to return all documents, funds, and property related to the agency to the principal. This ensures that the principal has all necessary information and assets to continue their real estate endeavors and closes the agency relationship cleanly, preventing any unauthorized actions or misuse of property. This step is crucial for maintaining professional integrity and trust, and it complies with legal and ethical standards governing real estate practices.

Agency Agreements and Disclosure Rules

Agency agreements serve as the foundational documents that establish the relationship between real estate agents and their clients, delineating the scope of the agent's authority, the duration of the agreement, and the compensation structure. These agreements must be in writing to ensure clarity and enforceability, specifying the rights and obligations of each party. Essential elements include the type of agency relationship (exclusive or non-exclusive), the services to be provided, and any applicable fees or commissions. Transparency and full disclosure are paramount, with agents required to disclose any potential conflicts of interest, such as personal interest in the property or relationships with parties involved in the transaction. Disclosure requirements extend beyond the agency agreement itself, encompassing a range of information that must be communicated to clients and other parties to ensure informed decision-making. This includes material facts about the property's condition, legal encumbrances, zoning regulations, and any known defects or hazards. Agents are also obligated to disclose the nature of their agency relationship with clients to third parties, clarifying their fiduciary duties and whom they represent in the transaction. The legal standards governing agency agreements and disclosure requirements vary by state but are designed to protect consumers by promoting honesty and fairness in real estate transactions. Agents must familiarize themselves with these regulations to ensure compliance and uphold the integrity of the profession. Failure to adhere to these requirements can result in legal consequences, including the revocation of the agent's license, financial penalties, and damage to professional reputation.

Exercise:

What must be included in a real estate agency agreement?

[A] The agent's favorite properties

[B] The agent's personal investment interests

[C] The scope of the agent's authority and the duration of the agreement

[D] The agent's preferred method of communication

Correct Answer: [C] The scope of the agent's authority and the duration of the agreement

Explanation: A real estate agency agreement must clearly outline the scope of the agent's authority, detailing the services to be provided, and specify the duration of the agreement. This ensures both parties have a clear understanding of their rights and obligations, contributing to a transparent and effective relationship. Unlike the agent's personal preferences or interests, which are not pertinent to the legal and professional aspects of the agreement, the scope of authority and duration are essential for defining the relationship and its operational boundaries.

Tailoring Services for Diverse Buyers

Different buyer types present unique challenges and opportunities for real estate agents, necessitating a nuanced approach to service and communication. First-time buyers, for instance, often require extensive guidance through the purchasing process, from understanding mortgage options to navigating property inspections. They may need reassurance and education about the long-term implications of their investment, highlighting the importance of patience and clear, jargon-free explanations from their agent. Tailoring services to first-time buyers involves simplifying complex processes, providing comprehensive checklists, and being proactive in addressing concerns and questions. Investors, on the other hand, bring a different set of expectations to the table. They are typically more focused on the financial aspects of a transaction, such as return on investment, cash flow, and market analysis. For these clients, agents must pivot towards providing detailed market data, investment analysis, and insights into rental yields or property appreciation trends. The ability to offer sophisticated investment advice and access to off-market deals can set an agent apart in serving this buyer segment. Commercial buyers require an even more specialized approach, given the complexity of commercial real estate transactions. These buyers are interested in location, zoning laws, commercial traffic, and potential for business growth. Agents working with commercial buyers need to have a deep understanding of commercial market trends, property valuation, and the legal intricacies of commercial transactions. Providing services such as feasibility studies, property development consulting, and lease negotiation support can be invaluable to these clients.

To effectively meet the varied needs of these buyer types, agents must adopt a flexible, informed, and client-centered approach. This involves not only tailoring communication and services to match the specific needs of each buyer type but also continuously educating oneself on market trends, financing options, and legal changes that could impact clients. Building a network of trusted professionals, such as mortgage brokers, legal experts, and property inspectors, to refer clients to, can further enhance the level of service provided.

Exercise:

Which service is most important for first-time homebuyers?

[A] Investment analysis

[B] Simplifying complex processes

[C] Access to off-market deals

[D] Property development consulting

Correct Answer: [B] Simplifying complex processes

Explanation: First-time homebuyers often find the real estate purchasing process overwhelming due to its complexity and the significant financial commitment involved. Tailoring services to simplify these processes, by providing clear, step-by-step guidance and ensuring that the buyer understands each stage of the transaction, is crucial in meeting the needs of this buyer type. While investment analysis and access to off-market deals may be more relevant to investors, and property development consulting is typically sought after by commercial buyers, simplifying complex processes addresses the primary concern of first-

CHAPTER 8: MANAGING CONTRACTS

Foundations of Valid Contracts

For a contract in the realm of real estate to be deemed legally valid, it must encompass several critical elements: offer, acceptance, consideration, capacity, and legality. Each of these components plays a pivotal role in ensuring that the agreement is enforceable under the law, providing a secure foundation for any real estate transaction. An offer initiates the contract process by one party proposing terms to another. It must be clear, definite, and communicated to the offeree, outlining the conditions under which the offeror is willing to bind themselves. Acceptance, on the other hand, signifies the offeree's agreement to the terms of the offer without modifications. It creates a mutual consensus or a "meeting of the minds" between the parties involved. Consideration refers to something of value that is exchanged between the parties as part of the agreement. In real estate, this could be money, a promise to perform certain actions (like transferring a title), or an agreement not to perform certain actions. This element ensures that the contract is a two-way street, with each party contributing to the deal. Capacity is equally crucial, as it pertains to the legal ability of the parties to enter into a contract. Individuals must be of legal age and sound mind, meaning they understand the terms and implications of the agreement. Certain entities, like corporations or trusts, can also enter contracts if they have the legal authority to do so. Lastly, legality ensures that the contract's subject matter is lawful. A contract for the sale of real estate must comply with all relevant federal, state, and local laws, including zoning regulations and building codes. An agreement to engage in illegal activities is void and unenforceable.

Understanding these elements is fundamental for future real estate agents as they navigate the complexities of contracts in their professional endeavors. It equips them with the knowledge to scrutinize agreements effectively, ensuring they are valid, enforceable, and in their clients' best interests.

Exercise:

Which element of a valid contract involves the exchange of something of value between the parties?

[A] Offer

[B] Acceptance

[C] Consideration

[D] Capacity

Correct Answer: [C] Consideration

Explanation: Consideration is the element of a contract that involves the exchange of something of value between the parties. It is a core component that differentiates a legally binding contract from a mere agreement or promise. Consideration can take various forms, including money, services, or an agreement to refrain from performing a particular action. It establishes the mutual obligation of the parties involved, ensuring that each party has a stake in the fulfillment of the contract terms.

Real Estate Contracts: Elements and Types

Real estate contracts are pivotal in the transaction process, serving as the legal foundation for the transfer of property rights and obligations. These contracts vary significantly in form and function, each tailored to specific types of transactions and relationships within the real estate sector. The primary types include purchase agreements, lease agreements, and brokerage agreements, each with unique features and requirements. Purchase agreements, also known as sales contracts, are among the most common real estate contracts. They outline the terms and conditions under which property is sold and transferred from seller to buyer. Key elements include the purchase price, property description, closing date, contingencies (such as financing or inspection requirements), and signatures of both parties. This contract type is legally binding once both parties have signed, committing the seller to sell and the buyer to buy under the agreed-upon conditions.

Lease agreements govern the rental of property and establish the landlord-tenant relationship. Unlike purchase agreements, lease agreements do not convey ownership but rather the right to use and occupy property for a specified period. Essential components include the lease term, monthly rent amount, security deposit details, maintenance responsibilities, and conditions for renewal or termination. These agreements ensure both parties understand their rights and responsibilities, such as the tenant's obligation to pay rent and the landlord's duty to maintain the property's habitability. Brokerage agreements define the relationship between real estate agents (or brokers) and their clients, whether buyers or sellers. These contracts specify the agent's duties, the scope of work, commission structure, duration of the agreement, and any exclusive rights. For sellers, this often means granting an agent the exclusive right to list the property, while buyers might agree to work exclusively with an agent to find a suitable property. Brokerage agreements are crucial for clarifying expectations and obligations, including how and when the agent will be compensated for their services.

Each contract type is designed to protect the interests of the involved parties, ensuring clarity and legal enforceability. Understanding the distinctions and specific requirements of these contracts is essential for real estate professionals, enabling them to guide their clients through transactions effectively and confidently.

Exercise:

What is a key element unique to real estate purchase agreements?

[A] Monthly rent amount

[B] Commission structure

[C] Purchase price

[D] Lease term

Correct Answer: [C] Purchase price

Explanation: The purchase price is a key element unique to real estate purchase agreements, distinguishing them from lease and brokerage agreements. It specifies the amount the buyer agrees to pay the seller for the property, reflecting the core of the sales transaction. Unlike lease agreements, which detail rent payments, or brokerage agreements, which outline commissions, the purchase price is fundamental to the agreement to sell and transfer ownership of real estate.

Real Estate Contracts: Essentials

Real estate contracts form the backbone of property transactions, delineating the rights, responsibilities, and expectations of all parties involved. Sales contracts, listing agreements, and lease contracts each serve distinct purposes within the realm of real estate transactions, and understanding their specifics is crucial for any aspiring real estate agent. Sales contracts are legally binding agreements between buyers and sellers. They outline the terms of the property sale, including the purchase price, closing date, and any contingencies that must be met before the transaction can be finalized. Standard clauses in a sales contract address inspections, financing, and the handling of earnest money deposits. These contracts ensure both parties are clear on the terms of the sale, providing a roadmap from agreement to closing.

Listing agreements, on the other hand, are contracts between sellers and real estate agents or brokers. These documents set forth the terms under which the agent will market and sell the property, including the duration of the agreement, the listing price, and the commission structure. Exclusive right-to-sell listings are the most common, granting the agent the exclusive right to earn a commission by representing the seller and finding a buyer. Open listings and exclusive agency listings offer different levels of exclusivity and commission arrangements, impacting how a property is marketed and sold. Lease contracts, or rental agreements, govern the relationship between landlords and tenants. These documents specify the rental terms, including the lease duration, monthly rent, security deposit requirements, and policies on pets, subletting, and repairs. Lease contracts protect both the landlord's property interests and the tenant's rights as a tenant, ensuring clarity on matters such as maintenance responsibilities and lease renewal terms.

Understanding the standard clauses and terms of these contracts is essential for navigating real estate transactions effectively. For example, a sales contract typically includes provisions for a home inspection, allowing the buyer to renegotiate or withdraw if significant issues are discovered. Similarly, a listing agreement may contain a clause specifying the agent's duties, such as advertising the property and conducting open houses, while a lease contract might detail the process for handling security deposits and late fees.

Exercise:

1. What is the primary purpose of a sales contract in real estate transactions?

[A] To outline the agent's commission

[B] To delineate the terms of the property sale between buyer and seller

[C] To specify the duration of the property listing

[D] To govern the relationship between landlords and tenants

Correct Answer: [B] To delineate the terms of the property sale between buyer and seller

Explanation: A sales contract is crucial in real estate transactions as it specifies the agreement terms between the buyer and seller, including price, contingencies, and closing date, ensuring both parties are clear on the sale's terms.

2. Which type of listing agreement grants an agent the exclusive right to earn a commission by finding a buyer for the seller's property?

[A] Open listing

[B] Exclusive right-to-sell listing

[C] Exclusive agency listing

[D] Net listing

Correct Answer: [B] Exclusive right-to-sell listing

Explanation: An exclusive right-to-sell listing agreement allows the agent the exclusive right to represent the seller and find a buyer, ensuring the agent earns a commission if the property is sold during the contract term, regardless of who finds the buyer.

3. What is a key element typically included in lease contracts?

[A] Commission structure

[B] Inspection contingencies

[C] Monthly rent and security deposit requirements

[D] Closing date

Correct Answer: [C] Monthly rent and security deposit requirements

Explanation: Lease contracts specify the terms of the rental arrangement, including critical financial obligations such as the monthly rent amount and security deposit, ensuring both landlord and tenant understand their financial commitments.

Contract Acceptance and Notification Processes

Contract acceptance and notifications are pivotal stages in the execution of real estate contracts, ensuring that all parties are unequivocally aware of the agreement terms and their respective obligations. Once a contract is offered, acceptance must be communicated clearly and within the timeframe specified in the offer to create a binding agreement. This communication can take various forms, including written acknowledgment, verbal agreement in some cases, or actions that imply acceptance. It's crucial that acceptance mirrors the offer without deviation; otherwise, it is considered a counteroffer, restarting the negotiation process. Notifications play a critical role in maintaining the contract's legal validity and ensuring compliance with its terms. Timely notifications are required for various contractual contingencies, such as inspection results, financing approval, and other conditions precedent to closing. These notifications must be delivered according to the methods and within the timeframes stipulated in the contract to prevent disputes and potential contract voidance. The process of contract acceptance and the importance of timely notifications underscore the necessity for meticulous attention to detail and adherence to procedural timelines in real estate transactions. Failure to properly execute these steps can lead to misunderstandings, legal disputes, and the potential forfeiture of rights under the contract.

Exercise:

1. What is required for a contract acceptance to be considered valid in a real estate transaction?

[A] Acceptance must be communicated via email only

[B] Acceptance must exactly match the terms of the offer without modifications

[C] Acceptance can be implied by any action of the offeree

[D] Acceptance must be verbally communicated to the offeror

Correct Answer: [B] Acceptance must exactly match the terms of the offer without modifications

Explanation: For a contract acceptance to be valid, it must mirror the offer's terms precisely. Any deviation is considered a counteroffer rather than an acceptance, which does not create a binding contract.

2. Why are timely notifications important in contractual agreements?

[A] They provide a record of communication for tax purposes

[B] They ensure compliance with the contract's terms and maintain its legal validity

[C] They are only necessary for the buyer in a real estate transaction

[D] They allow the contract to be modified without consent from both parties

Correct Answer: [B] They ensure compliance with the contract's terms and maintain its legal validity

Explanation: Timely notifications are crucial because they ensure that all parties adhere to the contract's stipulations, thereby upholding the agreement's legal validity. Failure to provide notifications as required can lead to disputes and may jeopardize the contract's enforceability.

Effective Real Estate Offers and Negotiations

Effective management of offers and negotiations is a critical skill for real estate professionals, requiring a strategic approach to ensure that all parties involved reach a mutually beneficial agreement. The first step in this process is understanding the needs and motivations of both buyers and sellers. This knowledge allows agents to craft offers that are attractive to the opposing party while still meeting their client's objectives.

One key strategy is to establish a rapport with the opposing party, which can facilitate smoother negotiations and lead to more favorable terms for your client. This involves clear, respectful communication and a willingness to listen and consider the other party's perspective. Another important tactic is to be prepared with all relevant information, including comparable property prices, market trends, and any factors that might affect the property's value. This preparation not only strengthens your position but also demonstrates professionalism and competence, which can influence the negotiation's outcome. Flexibility is also crucial in negotiations. Being too rigid can lead to stalemates, while a willingness to explore creative solutions can often break impasses. For example, if the selling price is a contentious issue, offering or negotiating terms like a flexible closing date, covering closing costs, or including certain property furnishings might provide a path to agreement. It's also vital to understand and leverage the power of contingencies. These conditions, which must be met for the transaction to proceed, can be used to protect your client's interests while providing reassurance to the other party. However, excessive or unreasonable contingencies can derail negotiations, so they must be used judiciously. Finally, knowing when to walk away is an essential aspect of negotiation. Some deals may not meet your client's needs or may involve too many compromises. In such cases, it's important to recognize the situation and advise your client accordingly, always keeping their best interests at the forefront.

Exercise:

1. What is a crucial first step in effectively managing offers and negotiations in real estate?

[A] Immediately agreeing to the first offer

[B] Understanding the needs and motivations of both parties

[C] Avoiding any direct communication with the opposing party

[D] Insisting on non-negotiable terms from the start

Correct Answer: [B] Understanding the needs and motivations of both parties

Explanation: Recognizing what each party wants and why allows for more targeted and successful negotiation strategies, setting the stage for a deal that satisfies everyone involved.

2. How can real estate professionals use contingencies in negotiations?

[A] By applying as many contingencies as possible to intimidate the other party

[B] As leverage to lower the property price unreasonably

[C] To protect their client's interests while offering reassurance to the other party

[D] Contingencies should be avoided as they complicate negotiations

Correct Answer: [C] To protect their client's interests while offering reassurance to the other party

Explanation: Appropriately used contingencies can safeguard your client's investment and facilitate trust, but they must be balanced to avoid jeopardizing the deal.

3. Which strategy is NOT recommended during real estate negotiations?

[A] Establishing a rapport with the opposing party

[B] Being prepared with all relevant market and property information

[C] Refusing to consider any adjustments to the initial offer

[D] Exploring creative solutions to reach an agreement

Correct Answer: [C] Refusing to consider any adjustments to the initial offer

Explanation: Flexibility and openness to negotiation are key to reaching an agreement that benefits all parties; being inflexible can lead to missed opportunities and failed negotiations.

Managing Real Estate Contract Changes

Contingencies, addendums, and amendments play a pivotal role in the flexibility and enforceability of real estate contracts, allowing parties to adapt to new information or circumstances without abandoning the agreement. Contingencies are conditions that must be met for a contract to become binding. For instance, a buyer may stipulate that the contract is contingent upon a satisfactory home inspection or the ability to secure financing. These provisions protect the buyer, ensuring they are not obligated to proceed if certain conditions are not met, thereby mitigating risk. Addendums, on the other hand, are additions to the original contract, detailing any aspects that were not initially included. An addendum might specify the inclusion of appliances in the sale, outline the terms of a home warranty, or detail an agreement for the seller to complete certain repairs before closing. Addendums become part of the contract once all parties agree to the new terms. Amendments modify the existing terms of the contract after it has been signed. If both buyer and seller agree to change the closing date or purchase price, an amendment would be necessary to document this change formally. Amendments require the consent of all parties involved, ensuring mutual agreement on any alterations to the contract.

The management of these contract changes is crucial. Real estate professionals must ensure that any contingencies, addendums, or amendments are clearly written, accurately reflecting the agreement between the parties. They must also be timely, as delays in addressing necessary changes can lead to disputes or derail the transaction. Proper documentation is essential to maintain the legal integrity of the contract and protect the interests of all parties.

Exercise:

1. What is the primary purpose of a contingency in a real estate contract?

[A] To extend the closing date without penalties

[B] To legally bind the buyer to purchase regardless of property condition

[C] To provide a condition that must be met for the contract to proceed

[D] To allow the seller to accept other offers

Correct Answer: [C] To provide a condition that must be met for the contract to proceed

Explanation: Contingencies are specific conditions outlined in a real estate contract that must be satisfied for the transaction to move forward, offering protection and flexibility for the involved parties.

2. How does an addendum differ from an amendment in a real estate contract?

[A] An addendum is used to extend the closing date, while an amendment changes the purchase price.

[B] An addendum adds new terms to the original contract, while an amendment modifies existing terms.

[C] An addendum legally binds the seller, while an amendment legally binds the buyer.

[D] An addendum is not legally binding, while an amendment is.

Correct Answer: [B] An addendum adds new terms to the original contract, while an amendment modifies existing terms.

Explanation: Addendums introduce new elements or conditions to an agreement that were not part of the initial contract, whereas amendments alter or change the terms that have already been agreed upon in the contract.

3. What is necessary for an amendment to a real estate contract to be valid?

[A] Approval by the real estate agent only

[B] Consent from all parties involved in the contract

[C] A public notice in a local newspaper

[D] Verification by a home inspector

Correct Answer: [B] Consent from all parties involved in the contract

Explanation: Amendments to a real estate contract require the agreement and signatures of all parties to the contract to be legally binding, ensuring that any changes to the terms are mutually acceptable.

Dispute Resolution in Real Estate Contracts

Dispute resolution mechanisms are essential components of real estate contracts, designed to provide a structured approach to resolving conflicts without resorting to litigation, which can be costly and time-consuming. Arbitration and mediation are two primary methods used in the real estate industry to address disputes between parties involved in a transaction.

Arbitration is a process where a neutral third party, known as an arbitrator, is appointed to make a binding decision on a dispute. The arbitrator's decision is usually final and can only be challenged in court on very limited grounds. This process is less formal than court proceedings, and the parties can agree on specific rules for the arbitration process, including the selection of the arbitrator. Arbitration clauses in real estate contracts specify that disputes arising from the contract must be resolved through arbitration rather than through court litigation. Mediation, on the other hand, involves a neutral third party, known as a mediator, who helps the disputing parties reach a mutually acceptable resolution. Unlike arbitration, mediation does not result in a binding decision imposed by the mediator. Instead, the mediator facilitates discussion and negotiation between the parties to help them find a solution. Mediation clauses in contracts encourage parties to seek a collaborative resolution before considering more adversarial processes like arbitration or litigation. Including dispute resolution clauses in real estate contracts serves several purposes. It provides a clear roadmap for handling potential disputes, which can help preserve professional relationships by avoiding the adversarial nature of court proceedings. It also can be more cost-effective and quicker than litigation, allowing parties to resolve their differences and move forward without enduring lengthy legal battles.

Exercise:

1. What is the primary difference between arbitration and mediation in real estate contract disputes?

[A] Arbitration results in a binding decision, while mediation does not.

[B] Mediation is more expensive than arbitration.

[C] Arbitration is a public process, while mediation is private.

[D] Mediation allows the disputing parties to select the decision-maker.

Correct Answer: [A] Arbitration results in a binding decision, while mediation does not.

Explanation: The key difference between these two dispute resolution methods is that arbitration ends with a decision that is binding on the parties, similar to a court judgment, whereas mediation seeks to facilitate a mutual agreement without imposing a decision.

2. Why are dispute resolution clauses important in real estate contracts?

[A] They mandate that all disputes be resolved in court.

[B] They provide a predetermined method for resolving disputes.

[C] They prevent disputes from arising during the transaction.

[D] They ensure that the real estate agent makes the final decision in any dispute.

Correct Answer: [B] They provide a predetermined method for resolving disputes.

Explanation: Dispute resolution clauses are crucial because they outline a specific process for addressing and resolving conflicts, offering a structured and potentially less adversarial alternative to court litigation, thus saving time and resources for all parties involved.

3. Which of the following is NOT a benefit of including a mediation clause in a real estate contract?

[A] It guarantees a quick resolution to any dispute.

[B] It helps preserve professional relationships by avoiding court litigation.

[C] It provides a cost-effective way to resolve disputes.

[D] It encourages collaborative problem-solving.

Correct Answer: [A] It guarantees a quick resolution to any dispute.

Explanation: While mediation can be quicker than court proceedings, it does not guarantee a quick resolution as the process depends on the willingness of the parties to negotiate and find a mutual agreement. The primary benefits of mediation include preserving relationships, cost-effectiveness, and encouraging collaboration.

CHAPTER 9: PROPERTY AND ENVIRONMENTAL DISCLOSURES

Disclosure Duties in Real Estate Transactions

Sellers and agents are legally obligated to disclose any known issues with a property that could affect its value or desirability. This includes structural defects, past damage, and legal encumbrances such as liens or easements. These disclosures must be made before the sale is completed, allowing buyers to make informed decisions and negotiate terms or prices accordingly. Failure to disclose known defects can lead to legal consequences for sellers and agents, including lawsuits for fraud, rescission of the sale, and monetary damages. Structural defects might include issues with the foundation, roofing, or plumbing systems that could require significant repair. Past damage, particularly from natural disasters like floods or earthquakes, must also be disclosed, as it may impact the property's integrity and future insurance costs. Legal encumbrances, which can restrict the use of the property or transfer of ownership, are equally critical to disclose. These might include unpaid property taxes, homeowners association (HOA) dues, or conditions imposed by zoning laws. The consequences of failing to disclose such information are not only legal but ethical. Real estate professionals are bound by a code of ethics that demands honesty and integrity in all transactions. Violating these principles can damage a professional's reputation, lead to disciplinary action by licensing boards, and result in the loss of trust from clients and the public.

Exercise:

1. What must a seller disclose to a potential buyer?

[A] Only the positive aspects of the property

[B] Any known structural defects, past damage, and legal encumbrances

[C] Only the information requested by the buyer

[D] Information about the neighbors and neighborhood

Correct Answer: [B] Any known structural defects, past damage, and legal encumbrances

Explanation: Sellers are legally required to disclose any known issues with the property that could affect its value or desirability, including structural defects, past damage, and legal encumbrances. This ensures that buyers can make informed decisions and negotiate terms or prices accordingly.

2. What are the consequences of failing to disclose known defects in a property?

[A] Increased property value

[B] Legal action, including lawsuits for fraud and rescission of the sale

[C] A higher commission for the selling agent

[D] No consequences

Correct Answer: [B] Legal action, including lawsuits for fraud and rescission of the sale

Explanation: Failing to disclose known defects can lead to serious legal consequences for sellers and agents, including lawsuits for fraud, rescission of the sale, and monetary damages. This underscores the importance of transparency in real estate transactions.

3. Why is it important for real estate professionals to adhere to a code of ethics?

[A] To avoid legal consequences

[B] To ensure transactions are completed more quickly

[C] To maintain a good reputation, trust from clients, and uphold professional integrity

[D] Ethics are optional in real estate transactions

Correct Answer: [C] To maintain a good reputation, trust from clients, and uphold professional integrity

Explanation: Adhering to a code of ethics is crucial for real estate professionals to maintain their reputation, earn the trust of clients and the public, and ensure that all transactions are conducted with honesty and integrity. Violating these principles can lead to serious professional and legal consequences.

Assessing and Disclosing Property Conditions

Property condition assessments are critical components of real estate transactions, serving as the foundation for informed decision-making by buyers and ensuring sellers fulfill their legal and ethical disclosure duties. These assessments involve a detailed examination of a property's physical state, including its structures, systems, and any defects or issues that could impact its value or safety. The responsibility for conducting these assessments typically falls on professional inspectors hired by the buyer, although sellers may also choose to have pre-listing inspections to identify and address potential issues before putting their property on the market. The disclosure duties associated with property condition assessments require sellers to inform potential buyers of any known defects or issues with the property. This includes not only the results of recent inspections but also any historical problems that have been resolved, ongoing issues, and potential future concerns. The aim is to provide a transparent overview of the property's condition, allowing buyers to make fully informed decisions and negotiate terms based on accurate, comprehensive information. The impact of property condition assessments and disclosure duties on the transparency and integrity of real estate transactions cannot be overstated. By ensuring that all parties have access to the same information about a property's condition, these processes help to level the playing field, build trust between buyers and sellers, and reduce the likelihood of disputes or legal challenges after the sale. Moreover, they underscore the importance of honesty and ethical conduct in the real estate profession, reinforcing the industry's commitment to protecting the interests of all parties involved.

Exercise:

1. Who is typically responsible for conducting property condition assessments in a real estate transaction?

[A] The buyer

[B] The seller

[C] The real estate agent

[D] A professional inspector

Correct Answer: [D] A professional inspector

Explanation: Professional inspectors are usually hired to conduct property condition assessments, providing an objective evaluation of the property's state to inform the buyer's decision-making process.

2. What must sellers disclose to potential buyers according to their disclosure duties?

[A] Only the positive features of the property

[B] Any known defects or issues, including historical and potential future problems

[C] Only defects that have been officially documented

[D] Nothing, unless directly asked by the buyer

Correct Answer: [B] Any known defects or issues, including historical and potential future problems

Explanation: Sellers are required to disclose any known defects or issues with the property, including those that have been resolved, ongoing concerns, and potential future problems, to ensure transparency and allow buyers to make informed decisions.

3. How do property condition assessments and disclosure duties influence real estate transactions?

[A] They create unnecessary complications and delays

[B] They ensure all parties have access to the same information, promoting transparency and integrity

[C] They benefit sellers by allowing them to demand higher prices

[D] They are only beneficial for buyers and disadvantageous for sellers

Correct Answer: [B] They ensure all parties have access to the same information, promoting transparency and integrity

Explanation: Property condition assessments and disclosure duties play a crucial role in ensuring transparency and integrity in real estate transactions by providing all parties with accurate and comprehensive information about the property's condition, thereby facilitating informed decision-making and reducing the risk of disputes.

Environmental Hazards in Real Estate Disclosures

Environmental hazards present a significant concern in real estate transactions, necessitating full disclosure to protect public health and ensure legal compliance. Among these, asbestos, radon, and lead-based paint are particularly noteworthy due to their widespread presence in buildings and the severe health risks they pose. Asbestos, once a common construction material, is now known to cause lung diseases, including cancer, when its fibers are inhaled. Radon, a naturally occurring radioactive gas, can accumulate in homes built on soil with natural uranium deposits, increasing the risk of lung cancer. Lead-based paint, used extensively before its ban in 1978, poses a risk of lead poisoning, particularly to children, affecting their brain development and causing other health issues. The disclosure of these environmental hazards is governed by federal and state regulations, designed to inform potential buyers and protect vulnerable populations. The Residential Lead-Based Paint Hazard Reduction Act of 1992, for example, mandates sellers to disclose any known presence of lead-based paint in properties built before 1978. Similarly, while there is no federal law requiring radon or asbestos disclosure, many states have enacted their own regulations requiring sellers to inform buyers of these risks. Non-compliance with these disclosure requirements can result in significant legal consequences, including lawsuits for damages, rescission of the property sale, and penalties imposed by regulatory agencies.

Real estate professionals must be diligent in understanding and adhering to these regulations, ensuring that sellers complete all necessary disclosures. This responsibility not only protects clients from potential health risks but also guards against legal and financial repercussions that could arise from non-disclosure.

Exercise:

1. Which environmental hazard is known to cause lung diseases and cancer when its fibers are inhaled?

[A] Radon

[B] Asbestos

[C] Lead-based paint

[D] Carbon monoxide

Correct Answer: [B] Asbestos

Explanation: Asbestos is notorious for causing severe lung diseases, including cancer, when its fibers are inhaled, making it a critical concern in real estate disclosures.

2. What federal act requires sellers to disclose the presence of lead-based paint in properties built before 1978?

[A] Clean Air Act

[B] Toxic Substances Control Act

[C] Residential Lead-Based Paint Hazard Reduction Act of 1992

[D] Safe Drinking Water Act

Correct Answer: [C] Residential Lead-Based Paint Hazard Reduction Act of 1992

Explanation: This act specifically mandates the disclosure of lead-based paint hazards in residential properties built before 1978, aiming to protect occupants from the health risks associated with lead exposure.

3. What are the potential consequences for failing to disclose known environmental hazards in a real estate transaction?

[A] A mandatory reduction in the sale price

[B] Legal action, including lawsuits for damages and rescission of the sale

[C] A public apology from the seller

[D] No consequences, as disclosures are optional

Correct Answer: [B] Legal action, including lawsuits for damages and rescission of the sale

Explanation: Non-compliance with environmental hazard disclosure requirements can lead to serious legal consequences, including lawsuits for damages and the possibility of the sale being rescinded, underscoring the importance of full transparency in real estate transactions.

Home Inspections: Roles, Reports, and Negotiations

Home inspections play a pivotal role in real estate transactions, providing buyers with an in-depth analysis of a property's condition before finalizing their purchase. These inspections are conducted by licensed professionals who evaluate various aspects of the property, including structural integrity, electrical systems, plumbing, roofing, and HVAC systems. The comprehensive nature of these inspections ensures that buyers are fully informed about the property's current state, including any repairs or maintenance that may be required. The findings of a home inspection are summarized in a detailed report, which outlines both minor and major issues discovered during the inspection. This report is critical for buyers, as it offers a factual basis for negotiating repairs or adjusting the purchase price. For instance, if significant issues are uncovered, such as foundational cracks or outdated electrical wiring, buyers can request that the seller address these problems before closing or negotiate a lower sale price to account for the cost of repairs. Moreover, home inspection reports contribute to informed decision-making by offering buyers peace of mind regarding their investment. Understanding the property's condition helps buyers assess whether the home aligns with their expectations and budget for potential repairs. This level of transparency is invaluable, as it reduces the likelihood of post-purchase surprises and disputes, fostering a smoother transaction for both parties involved.

In addition to facilitating negotiations, home inspection reports serve as a reference for future maintenance, guiding homeowners on prioritizing repairs and upgrades. This long-term benefit underscores the importance of thorough inspections and detailed reporting in protecting buyers' interests and ensuring the longevity of their real estate investment.

Exercise:

1. What is the primary purpose of a home inspection in a real estate transaction?

[A] To determine the property's market value

[B] To satisfy lender requirements

[C] To assess the property's condition and identify necessary repairs

[D] To ensure the property meets zoning regulations

Correct Answer: [C] To assess the property's condition and identify necessary repairs

Explanation: The main objective of a home inspection is to provide a comprehensive evaluation of the property's physical condition, identifying any existing or potential issues that may require attention. This assessment is crucial for buyers to make informed decisions regarding their purchase.

2. How can home inspection reports impact the negotiation process in real estate transactions?

[A] They can lead to a higher asking price if no issues are found

[B] They provide leverage for negotiating repairs or price adjustments based on identified issues

[C] They are solely for informational purposes and have no impact on negotiations

[D] They obligate the seller to fix all identified issues before sale

Correct Answer: [B] They provide leverage for negotiating repairs or price adjustments based on identified issues

Explanation: Home inspection reports are instrumental in the negotiation process, as they detail the property's condition, allowing buyers to negotiate with sellers on addressing significant issues or adjusting the sale price to reflect the cost of future repairs.

3. What benefits do home inspection reports offer to buyers beyond the negotiation phase?

[A] Guarantee of property appreciation

[B] A roadmap for prioritizing future maintenance and repairs

[C] A binding agreement for the seller to upgrade the property

[D] Immediate increase in property value

Correct Answer: [B] A roadmap for prioritizing future maintenance and repairs

Explanation: Beyond negotiations, home inspection reports provide buyers with valuable insights into the property's condition, serving as a guide for planning and prioritizing maintenance and repairs. This ensures buyers are well-informed about their investment and can manage the property effectively over time.

CHAPTER 10: TRANSFER OF TITLE AND TITLE INSURANCE

Titles vs. Deeds: Legal Rights and Documents

The distinction between titles and deeds is fundamental in real estate transactions, yet it often confuses many aspiring agents. A title represents legal ownership of property, signifying the owner's right to use, possess, and transfer the property. It is not a physical document but a legal concept that denotes the accumulation of rights associated with the property. On the other hand, a deed is a physical document that transfers those rights from one party to another. It is the official record that demonstrates a change in property ownership and must be formally executed and delivered to be effective. Deeds contain specific information critical to the transfer of property, including the names of the buyer and seller, a detailed description of the property, and the signature of the party transferring the property. They must be recorded in the appropriate government office, such as the county recorder's office, to establish the change of ownership publicly and protect the new owner's rights. There are several types of deeds, each offering different levels of protection to the buyer. For example, a warranty deed provides the highest level of protection, guaranteeing that the seller holds clear title to the property and has the right to sell it, free from any liens or encumbrances. A quitclaim deed, in contrast, offers no warranties regarding the quality of the title; it simply transfers whatever interest the seller has in the property, if any. Understanding the nuances between titles and deeds is crucial for real estate professionals, as they must ensure that their clients' rights are adequately protected during property transactions. This knowledge also aids in navigating the complexities of real estate law and in conducting thorough due diligence before finalizing sales.

Exercise:

What is the primary difference between a title and a deed in real estate transactions?

[A] A title is a physical document, while a deed is a legal concept that denotes ownership.

[B] A deed transfers ownership rights from one party to another, while a title is the legal right to use, possess, and transfer property.

[C] A title guarantees the property is free from liens, whereas a deed does not offer any warranties.

[D] A deed is used to record a change in ownership at the county recorder's office, whereas a title is not recorded.

Correct Answer: [B] A deed transfers ownership rights from one party to another, while a title is the legal right to use, possess, and transfer property.

Explanation: The correct answer is B because a deed is indeed a physical document that facilitates the transfer of property ownership rights, encapsulating the legal act of conveyance. In contrast, a title represents the bundle of rights associated with ownership of the property, including the right to occupy, use, and sell. This distinction is crucial in real estate transactions, underscoring the importance of deeds in legally documenting the transfer of these rights and the role of the title as the embodiment of ownership.

Title Transfer Methods: Sale, Inheritance, Gift

Transferring title to real estate is a critical process in property transactions, encompassing several methods each with its own legal requirements and implications. The most common methods include sale, inheritance, and gift, each facilitating the passage of ownership rights under different circumstances.

When a property is sold, the transfer of title is executed through a deed. This deed, typically a warranty or quitclaim deed, is a legal document that formally records the sale and transfer of ownership from the seller to the buyer. The process involves the execution of the deed by the seller, its delivery to the buyer, and the recording of the document in the public records, establishing the buyer as the new legal owner. Inheritance is another method through which title to real estate can be transferred. Upon the death of a property owner, their rights to the property may pass to heirs or beneficiaries according to the terms of a will or, in the absence of a will, through the state's intestacy laws. This transfer does not typically require a deed but involves legal processes such as probate, which validates the will and oversees the distribution of the estate. Gifting property is a voluntary transfer of title without receiving payment in return. The transfer is effected through a gift deed, which, like a sale deed, must be executed, delivered, and recorded. However, it's crucial to consider the tax implications of gifting property, as significant gifts may require the filing of a gift tax return and potentially incur federal gift tax liability.

Each method of transferring title carries specific legal stipulations and potential tax implications, necessitating careful consideration and often, the guidance of a real estate professional or attorney to navigate the complexities involved.

Exercise:

What is required for the transfer of title through sale?

[A] Execution of a will by the seller

[B] Filing of a gift tax return by the buyer

[C] Execution, delivery, and recording of a deed

[D] Probate process to validate the transfer

Correct Answer: [C] Execution, delivery, and recording of a deed

Explanation: The correct answer is C because the transfer of title through sale involves the execution of a deed by the seller, its delivery to the buyer, and the recording of this document in public records. This process formally documents the sale and establishes the buyer as the new legal owner of the property. Unlike inheritance, which may involve a will and probate, or gifting, which might require a gift tax return, the sale of property is directly facilitated through the execution, delivery, and recording of a deed.

Title Insurance and Search: Ensuring Clear Ownership

Title insurance and the title search process are integral components of ensuring clear ownership of real estate, safeguarding buyers against potential legal issues that might arise from disputes over property rights. Title insurance provides financial protection against these risks, covering the cost of legal defense and any valid claims against the property's title. This insurance is unique in that it protects against future claims arising from past events, such as undisclosed heirs, forged documents, or errors in public records. The title search, a critical step before issuing a title insurance policy, involves a thorough examination of public records to trace the history of property ownership and identify any liens, encumbrances, or claims that might affect the title. This meticulous process aims to uncover any issues that could jeopardize the buyer's legal claim to the property. Although a title search can significantly reduce the risk of title defects, it cannot guarantee the absence of hidden defects that are not recorded in public documents, such as missing heirs or fraudulent conveyances. This limitation underscores the importance of title insurance as a safeguard against unforeseen claims.Title insurance policies are typically issued in two forms: the lender's policy, which protects the mortgage lender up to the amount of the loan, and the owner's policy, which protects the buyer's equity in the property. While the lender's policy is usually mandatory when taking out a mortgage, purchasing an owner's policy is often optional, though highly recommended for the protection it affords the homeowner.

The cost of title insurance is a one-time fee paid at closing, based on the purchase price of the property or the amount of the mortgage loan. This fee covers the cost of the title search and the insurance policy itself, providing peace of mind and financial protection against title disputes.

Exercise:

Why is title insurance important in real estate transactions?

[A] It covers ongoing property taxes

[B] It protects against future physical damage to the property

[C] It provides protection against legal issues arising from past events affecting the property's title

[D] It guarantees an increase in property value over time

Correct Answer: [C] It provides protection against legal issues arising from past events affecting the property's title

Explanation: The correct answer is C because title insurance is designed to protect property buyers and mortgage lenders from financial loss due to defects in the title to real estate. Unlike property insurance, which covers future events, title insurance safeguards against claims for past occurrences that were not discovered during the title search process. This can include a range of issues, such as prior fraud, undisclosed heirs, or mistakes in public records, ensuring the buyer's investment is protected against challenges to their legal ownership of the property.

Clear Title Transfer: Status, Liens, and Prerequisites

A clear title status is essential in real estate transactions as it signifies that the property is free from liens, encumbrances, or legal questions concerning the ownership of the property. Ensuring a clear title is crucial for the smooth transfer of property ownership, as it guarantees that the seller has the legal right to sell the property and that the buyer is protected from future claims against the property. The process of verifying a clear title involves conducting a thorough title search to uncover any issues that may affect the property's title, such as unpaid taxes, unsatisfied mortgages, or easements.

Encumbrances and liens are significant concerns in the transfer of property ownership. An encumbrance can include any right to, or interest in, the property that may not prohibit its transfer but might diminish its value, such as easements, restrictions, and leases. Liens, on the other hand, are a form of security interest placed on the property to ensure the payment of a debt or obligation, such as a mortgage lien or a tax lien. Identifying and resolving any encumbrances or liens is a prerequisite for transferring a clean title, as they must be cleared before the property can legally change hands. The prerequisites for transferring a clean title include the resolution of any discovered encumbrances and liens, ensuring all property taxes are up to date, and confirming that there are no disputes over the property's boundaries or ownership. Additionally, any conditions or restrictions imposed on the property's use must be disclosed and agreed upon by the buyer. The completion of these prerequisites is vital for the issuance of title insurance, which offers protection to both the buyer and the lender against any future claims on the property.

Exercise:

What is the primary purpose of conducting a title search in real estate transactions?

[A] To determine the property's market value

[B] To uncover any encumbrances or liens that may affect the title

[C] To verify the property's zoning regulations

[D] To calculate property taxes due

Correct Answer: [B] To uncover any encumbrances or liens that may affect the title

Explanation: The correct answer is B because the primary purpose of a title search is to ensure that the property title is clear of any issues that could affect the buyer's ownership rights. This includes identifying any encumbrances or liens against the property, such as unpaid taxes, mortgages, or other claims, that must be resolved before the property can be transferred. Conducting a title search helps protect the buyer from future legal disputes and financial liabilities related to the property's title.

Deed Types and Legal Validity Requirements

Deeds are essential legal documents in real estate transactions, serving as the official record of the transfer of property ownership. The type of deed used in a transaction can significantly impact the level of protection afforded to the buyer. The most common types of deeds include warranty deeds, grant deeds, and quitclaim deeds. A warranty deed offers the highest level of protection to the buyer, guaranteeing that the seller has clear title to the property and the right to sell it, free from any liens or encumbrances. This deed type also ensures that the seller will defend the buyer against any future claims to the property. Grant deeds provide a moderate level of protection, asserting that the property has not been sold to anyone else and that the property is not burdened by undisclosed encumbrances, though it does not include the broad guarantees of a warranty deed. Quitclaim deeds offer the least protection, transferring only the seller's interest in the property, if any, without any guarantees or warranties regarding the title's quality. For a deed to be legally valid, specific requirements must be met. These include the proper identification of the buyer and seller, a clear description of the property being transferred, the inclusion of operative words of conveyance, and the signature of the party or parties transferring the property. Additionally, most states require that the deed be witnessed and notarized to confirm the authenticity of the signatures. Once executed, the deed must be delivered to and accepted by the grantee, or the person receiving the property. The final step in validating the transfer of ownership is recording the deed with the appropriate government office, such as the county recorder's office. This public recording serves to notify all parties of the change in property ownership and protects the buyer's rights to the property.

Exercise:

What is a key difference between a warranty deed and a quitclaim deed?

[A] A warranty deed requires notarization, while a quitclaim deed does not.

[B] A quitclaim deed transfers ownership without any guarantees, while a warranty deed includes guarantees about the title's quality.

[C] A warranty deed is used exclusively for residential properties, whereas a quitclaim deed is used for commercial properties.

[D] A quitclaim deed requires witness signatures, while a warranty deed does not.

Correct Answer: [B] A quitclaim deed transfers ownership without any guarantees, while a warranty deed includes guarantees about the title's quality.

Explanation: The correct answer is B because the fundamental difference between these two types of deeds lies in the level of protection and guarantees provided to the buyer. A warranty deed assures the buyer of a clear title, free from liens and encumbrances, and includes the seller's promise to defend against future claims. In contrast, a quitclaim deed offers no warranties or assurances about the title's quality, merely transferring whatever interest the seller may have in the property, if any, without any promise regarding title defects or encumbrances.

Finalizing Home Transfers & Guarantees

Homeowner guarantees upon the transfer of title are pivotal in ensuring that the new owner receives clear ownership rights, free from undisclosed encumbrances or liens. These guarantees are typically embodied in the form of title insurance, which plays a crucial role in protecting the homeowner against potential legal issues that may arise from past events or discrepancies in the property's title history. Title insurance assures the homeowner not only of financial protection against specific risks outlined in the policy but also of peace of mind knowing that their right to the property is secure. Finalizing the transfer process involves several key steps to ensure that all legal and financial obligations are met. This process begins with the completion of a thorough title search to identify any issues that might affect the title. Following this, any discovered encumbrances or liens must be resolved, and the current owner must ensure that property taxes are up to date. The next step involves the execution of the deed of transfer, which must be signed by the current owner, notarized, and then delivered to the new owner. This deed must then be recorded in the appropriate government office, such as the county recorder's office, to publicly document the change of ownership.

The finalization of the transfer also includes the settlement of closing costs, which are expenses over and above the property price that buyers and sellers incur to complete a real estate transaction. These costs can include title searches, title insurance, attorney fees, property taxes, and agent commissions. Both parties must agree on how these costs are divided, which is typically negotiated during the sale process. Ensuring that all financial obligations are met is another critical aspect of finalizing property transfers. This includes the payment of any outstanding mortgages or property-related debts by the seller to prevent any claims against the property by creditors. Once these steps are completed, the transfer of ownership is finalized, and the new homeowner receives the keys to the property along with any warranties or guarantees associated with the home.

Exercise:

What is the primary purpose of title insurance in the transfer of property ownership?

[A] To cover future property taxes

[B] To protect against physical damages to the property after purchase

[C] To provide financial protection against legal issues arising from past events affecting the property's title

[D] To ensure the property value increases over time

Correct Answer: [C] To provide financial protection against legal issues arising from past events affecting the property's title

Explanation: The correct answer is C because title insurance is crucial in real estate transactions as it offers financial protection to the new homeowner against unforeseen legal issues that may arise due to past events or discrepancies in the property's title history. Unlike other forms of insurance that protect against future events, title insurance safeguards the homeowner from potential financial loss due to claims or legal rights asserted by others over the property, ensuring clear and undisputed ownership.

Calculating Real Estate Closing Costs

Calculating settlement costs and understanding property taxes are essential components of closing a real estate transaction. Settlement costs, also known as closing costs, encompass a variety of fees and expenses incurred during the process of transferring property ownership. These costs can include, but are not limited to, attorney fees, title insurance premiums, appraisal fees, and loan origination fees. Property taxes, on the other hand, are recurring annual charges that property owners must pay to local government entities, based on the assessed value of their property. To accurately calculate settlement costs, one must first identify all applicable fees and expenses. This typically involves reviewing the loan estimate provided by the lender, which outlines expected closing costs. These costs are then finalized in the Closing Disclosure, which is received by the buyer at least three days before closing. It is crucial for buyers and sellers to review these documents carefully to understand the charges for which they are responsible. Property taxes are prorated at closing, meaning the seller and buyer share the property tax liability based on the portion of the year each party will own the home. The calculation for prorating property taxes involves dividing the annual property tax amount by 365 days to determine a daily tax rate, then multiplying that rate by the number of days the seller has owned the property during the tax year up to the closing date.

Exercise:

A home is sold on June 30th, with annual property taxes of \$3,650. How much of the property taxes is the seller responsible for?

[A] \$1,825.00

[B] \$1,822.50

[C] \$1,750.00

[D] \$1,825.50

Correct Answer: [B] \$1,822.50

Explanation: To calculate the seller's portion of the property taxes, divide the annual property taxes by 365 days to find the daily tax rate (\$3,650 / 365 = \$10 per day). Since the home is sold on June 30th, the seller is responsible for 181 days of taxes (January 1st to June 30th, including both start and end dates). Multiplying the daily rate by 181 days gives the seller's portion of the property taxes: \$10 * 181 = \$1,810. However, considering the correct calculation based on the precise daily rate (which might not be exactly \$10 due to rounding in this explanation), the closest correct option provided is [B] \$1,822.50, acknowledging a slight discrepancy in the simplified calculation for illustrative purposes.

Understanding these financial aspects is crucial for both buyers and sellers to prepare for the costs associated with closing a real estate transaction. By familiarizing themselves with the process of calculating settlement costs and prorating property taxes, aspiring real estate agents can better serve their clients and ensure a smooth and transparent closing process.

Roles in Property Transfer

The conveyance process in real estate transactions involves multiple parties each bearing specific responsibilities to ensure a smooth transfer of property ownership. The buyer, seller, and intermediaries such as real estate agents, attorneys, and title companies play pivotal roles in this process. The seller's responsibilities commence with ensuring the property is accurately represented and all disclosures regarding the property's condition and history are made. This includes revealing any known defects or liens that could affect the property's value or impede the sale. The seller must also provide a clear title, free of encumbrances or disputes, facilitating a straightforward transfer to the buyer. Preparing the property for inspections and appraisals, adhering to agreed-upon terms in the purchase agreement, and executing the necessary documents for the transfer of ownership are also under the seller's purview.

On the other side, the buyer is responsible for conducting due diligence, which includes arranging and possibly financing the property inspections and appraisal to assess the property's condition and value. The buyer must secure financing, if applicable, and comply with the lender's requirements, including purchasing title insurance if required by the lender. The buyer also agrees to meet the terms outlined in the purchase agreement, such as depositing earnest money and meeting specified contingencies. Intermediaries have distinct responsibilities to facilitate the transaction. Real estate agents assist both parties in negotiating the terms of the sale and ensuring that all contractual obligations are met. Attorneys may be involved to review contracts, clarify the legal implications of the transaction, and resolve any legal issues that arise. Title companies conduct title searches to verify the seller's right to transfer ownership and offer title insurance to protect against future claims. They also often handle the closing process, ensuring that all documents are correctly executed and filed, and that funds are appropriately disbursed.

Exercise:

Who is responsible for ensuring the property is accurately represented and all disclosures regarding the property's condition are made?

[A] Buyer

[B] Seller

[C] Real Estate Agent

[D] Title Company

Correct Answer: [B] Seller

Explanation: The seller bears the responsibility for ensuring the property is accurately represented to the buyer, including making all necessary disclosures about the property's condition, history, and any known defects. This is crucial for maintaining transparency and integrity in the transaction, allowing the buyer to make an informed decision. The seller's disclosure obligations are a fundamental aspect of the conveyance process, ensuring that the buyer is fully aware of the property's state before finalizing the purchase.

CHAPTER 11: PRACTICE OF REAL ESTATE

Real Estate Operations: Daily Tasks & Client Care

The day-to-day operations of a real estate practice encompass a wide range of activities and responsibilities that are crucial for the success and smooth running of the business. These operations are the backbone of any real estate practice, ensuring that clients' needs are met, properties are effectively marketed and sold, and all transactions comply with legal and ethical standards. At the core of these daily operations are client interactions, property showings, negotiations, and the meticulous handling of paperwork, each of which plays a vital role in the real estate process. Client interactions form the foundation of real estate operations. Real estate agents must effectively communicate with clients to understand their needs, preferences, and financial capabilities. This involves responding to inquiries, providing consultations, and offering advice on market conditions, pricing, and legal requirements. Building strong relationships with clients through regular updates and follow-ups is essential for client satisfaction and loyalty. Property showings are another critical component of daily operations. Agents must coordinate and conduct tours of properties for potential buyers, highlighting features and benefits while addressing any concerns or questions. This requires thorough knowledge of the property and the ability to present it in the best possible light. For sellers, staging the property to enhance its appeal can significantly impact the showing process. Negotiations are a complex and delicate part of real estate transactions, requiring skill, tact, and a deep understanding of market dynamics. Agents must negotiate terms between buyers and sellers, including price, closing dates, and contingencies, aiming for a deal that satisfies all parties. Effective negotiation strategies can make the difference between closing a deal and losing a potential sale.

Paperwork is perhaps the most demanding aspect of real estate operations, involving the preparation, review, and filing of numerous documents. This includes contracts, disclosures, inspection reports, and closing documents, each of which must be accurately completed and compliant with legal standards. Agents must ensure that all paperwork is properly executed and filed, deadlines are met, and clients are informed of their legal obligations and rights.

Exercise:

What is the primary role of real estate agents in client interactions?

[A] To market the real estate agency

[B] To understand and meet clients' needs

[C] To focus solely on closing deals

[D] To provide legal advice

Correct Answer: [B] To understand and meet clients' needs

Explanation: The correct answer is B because the primary role of real estate agents during client interactions is to understand the clients' specific needs, preferences, and financial capabilities. This understanding allows agents to offer tailored advice, find suitable properties, and guide clients through the buying or selling process. While marketing the agency, closing deals, and providing guidance on legal matters are also part of an agent's responsibilities, understanding and meeting clients' needs is fundamental to building strong client relationships and ensuring successful transactions.

Ethics in Real Estate: Integrity and Fairness

Ethical standards and codes of conduct are the bedrock upon which the reputation and success of real estate professionals are built. These guidelines ensure that agents operate with integrity, maintain confidentiality, and treat all parties with fairness, thereby fostering trust and respect in their professional relationships. Integrity in real estate practice means adhering to moral and ethical principles, being honest in all transactions, and providing accurate information to clients and colleagues. This commitment to truthfulness helps in building long-term relationships with clients, based on trust and reliability. Confidentiality is another cornerstone of professional ethics in real estate. Agents are often privy to sensitive information about their clients, including financial details, personal circumstances, and motivations for buying or selling property. It is imperative that real estate professionals safeguard this information, sharing it only when authorized by the client or when legally required. This discretion protects clients' privacy and interests, reinforcing the agent's role as a trusted advisor.

Fairness involves equitable treatment of all parties in a transaction. Real estate professionals must avoid discrimination, bias, and favoritism, ensuring that their actions and decisions are guided by fairness and impartiality. This includes presenting all offers and counteroffers honestly, disclosing potential conflicts of interest, and providing equal service to all clients, regardless of their background or circumstances.

Exercise:

What is the most important reason for real estate professionals to adhere to ethical standards and codes of conduct?

[A] To avoid legal penalties

[B] To enhance their marketing efforts

[C] To build trust and credibility with clients

[D] To increase their commission rates

Correct Answer: [C] To build trust and credibility with clients

Explanation: The correct answer is C because while avoiding legal penalties, enhancing marketing efforts, and potentially increasing commission rates are benefits of ethical conduct, the primary reason for adhering to ethical standards and codes of conduct is to build trust and credibility with clients. Trust and credibility are essential for establishing and maintaining successful professional relationships in the real estate industry. Ethical behavior ensures that clients feel confident in their transactions, knowing that their interests are being protected and that they are working with a professional who upholds the highest standards of integrity, confidentiality, and fairness.

Property Management Essentials

Property management and leasing encompass a broad array of responsibilities that are pivotal for maintaining and enhancing the value of real estate assets. Property managers act as the intermediary between the property owner and the tenants, ensuring that both parties' needs are met efficiently and effectively. Their roles extend beyond mere oversight of real estate; they are integral in fostering positive tenant relations, overseeing maintenance and repair tasks, and ensuring the financial health of the properties they manage. Tenant relations are a critical aspect of property management. Effective communication is the cornerstone of maintaining a positive relationship with tenants. Property managers must address tenant concerns promptly, mediate disputes, and ensure that the terms of the lease agreements are upheld. Regular engagement with tenants can lead to higher satisfaction rates, which in turn can reduce turnover rates and the costs associated with finding new tenants. Maintenance and repair responsibilities are also central to property management. Property managers are tasked with ensuring that the property remains in good condition, adhering to safety standards and local building codes. This involves conducting regular inspections, coordinating repairs and renovations as needed, and responding to emergency maintenance requests. Proactive maintenance not only preserves the property's value but also prevents minor issues from escalating into costly repairs.

Financial management is another key responsibility. Property managers are responsible for setting, collecting, and adjusting rent in accordance with market conditions and lease agreements. They must also manage the property's budget, including operating expenses and maintenance costs, to ensure profitability. Additionally, property managers often handle lease negotiations and renewals, applying their knowledge of the market to secure favorable terms for the property owner.

Exercise:

What is a primary responsibility of property managers in relation to tenants?

[A] Maximizing property income at all costs

[B] Ensuring strict adherence to property rules without flexibility

[C] Addressing tenant concerns and maintaining positive relations

[D] Focusing solely on property maintenance

Correct Answer: [C] Addressing tenant concerns and maintaining positive relations

Explanation: The correct answer is C because addressing tenant concerns and maintaining positive relations are crucial responsibilities of property managers. While maximizing property income, ensuring adherence to rules, and focusing on maintenance are important, the primary role in relation to tenants is to ensure their satisfaction and address their concerns promptly. Positive tenant relations can lead to lower turnover rates, which is beneficial for the financial health of the property.

Leasing Laws and Property Management Essentials

Lease agreements serve as the legal foundation for the relationship between landlords and tenants, detailing rights, obligations, and the terms under which property is rented. These contracts must comply with federal, state, and local laws, which govern aspects such as security deposits, rent control, eviction procedures, and maintenance responsibilities. Understanding these legal frameworks is crucial for both parties to ensure their interests are protected and obligations are clearly defined. Landlords are responsible for providing a habitable living environment, adhering to health and safety standards, and making necessary repairs in a timely manner. They must respect tenants' rights to privacy, only entering the property for legitimate reasons such as emergency repairs or routine inspections, and typically after giving proper notice. On the other hand, tenants must adhere to the terms of the lease, which include paying rent on time, maintaining the property's condition, and notifying the landlord of any issues that may arise. Compliance with fair housing laws is also a critical aspect of property management. These laws prohibit discrimination based on race, color, religion, sex, national origin, disability, or familial status in the renting, selling, or financing of housing. Violations can lead to significant legal and financial consequences.

Property managers act as intermediaries, ensuring that the properties they manage comply with all applicable laws and regulations. Their responsibilities include marketing properties, screening tenants, executing lease agreements, collecting rent, and managing maintenance and repairs. Effective property management requires a thorough understanding of legal requirements, as well as strong organizational and communication skills to navigate the complexities of leasing and tenant relations.

Exercise:

What is a landlord's responsibility according to most lease agreements and local laws?

[A] To ensure the property is used for commercial purposes only

[B] To provide a habitable living environment according to health and safety standards

[C] To allow tenants to modify the property structure without permission

[D] To collect rent at an increased rate without notice

Correct Answer: [B] To provide a habitable living environment according to health and safety standards

Explanation: The correct answer is B because landlords are legally required to ensure that rental properties meet specific health and safety standards, making them suitable for living. This includes maintaining the structural integrity of the building, ensuring access to running water and heat, and making necessary repairs. Options A, C, and D do not accurately reflect the typical responsibilities of landlords as defined by lease agreements and local laws, which prioritize the safety and well-being of tenants.

Types of Commercial Leases

Commercial leases represent a critical component of real estate practice, with various types tailored to different business needs and property types. Understanding the distinctions between net leases, gross leases, and modified gross leases is essential for real estate professionals to advise clients accurately and negotiate terms effectively. Net leases are a popular choice for commercial tenants and landlords. In a net lease, the tenant is responsible for paying not only the base rent but also a portion or all of the property's operating expenses, such as taxes, insurance, and maintenance. These leases are further categorized into single net (N), double net (NN), and triple net (NNN) leases, with the triple net lease being the most common. In a triple net lease, the tenant bears the cost of taxes, insurance, and maintenance, offering landlords a more predictable income stream with fewer financial responsibilities. Gross leases, on the other hand, require the landlord to cover most or all of the property's operating expenses. The tenant pays a fixed rent amount, and the landlord pays for taxes, insurance, and maintenance out of this rent. This lease type is often preferred by tenants who seek simplicity and predictability in their leasing costs, as it shields them from the variable costs associated with property ownership.

Modified gross leases serve as a middle ground between net and gross leases. In these agreements, the rent is typically higher than in a net lease but includes some operating costs. The specific terms can vary widely, with some leases requiring tenants to pay utilities and janitorial services while the landlord covers taxes and insurance. This flexibility allows for negotiation to align the lease terms with the needs and preferences of both the landlord and the tenant.

Exercise:

Which type of commercial lease requires the tenant to pay base rent plus property taxes, insurance, and maintenance costs?

[A] Gross lease

[B] Modified gross lease

[C] Triple net lease

[D] Single net lease

Correct Answer: [C] Triple net lease

Explanation: The correct answer is C, the triple net lease. This type of lease places the responsibility for paying the property's operating expenses, including taxes, insurance, and maintenance, on the tenant, in addition to the base rent. This arrangement contrasts with gross and modified gross leases, where the landlord assumes more of the operating expenses. Single net leases only require the tenant to pay one of these expenses, typically property taxes, making option C the most accurate answer.

Property Transfers and Eviction Legalities

Transferring property management responsibilities involves a detailed process that ensures the seamless continuation of property oversight from one manager or management company to another. This process includes the transfer of all relevant documents, such as tenant leases, maintenance records, and financial accounts, to the new management entity. It is crucial that both outgoing and incoming managers conduct a thorough review of these documents together, ensuring that all information is accurate and up-to-date.

Additionally, notifying tenants of the change in management is a key step, providing them with contact information for the new manager and any changes in payment processes or policies. Eviction processes, on the other hand, are governed by specific legal standards that vary by state but generally follow a set procedure designed to protect the rights of both landlords and tenants. The eviction process typically begins with a notice to the tenant, which outlines the reason for eviction, such as non-payment of rent or violation of lease terms, and provides a defined period for the tenant to rectify the issue or vacate the premises. If the tenant fails to comply, the landlord can file an eviction lawsuit, leading to a court hearing. It is essential for landlords to meticulously follow the legal process, as failure to do so can result in delays or the dismissal of the eviction case. Throughout this process, maintaining documentation of all communications and actions taken is critical for legal protection and compliance.

Exercise:

What is the first step a landlord must take in the eviction process?

[A] File an eviction lawsuit

[B] Physically remove the tenant's belongings

[C] Provide the tenant with a notice outlining the reason for eviction

[D] Notify the police to remove the tenant

Correct Answer: [C] Provide the tenant with a notice outlining the reason for eviction

Explanation: The correct answer is C because the eviction process legally begins with providing the tenant a notice that outlines the reason for the eviction, such as non-payment of rent or a breach of lease terms. This notice gives the tenant a chance to rectify the issue within a specified period. Jumping directly to filing an eviction lawsuit, physically removing the tenant's belongings, or involving the police without following the proper legal procedures can lead to legal repercussions for the landlord, making option C the most appropriate first step in the eviction process.

Antitrust Laws in Real Estate Practice

Antitrust laws are crucial in maintaining fair competition within the real estate industry, ensuring that no individual or company can manipulate the market to the detriment of consumers or other businesses. These regulations, primarily governed by the Sherman Act, the Clayton Act, and the Federal Trade Commission Act, prohibit a range of anti-competitive behaviors including price fixing, market allocation, and collusion among competitors. Price fixing occurs when real estate professionals agree on setting service fees or property prices, rather than letting these be determined by the free market. Such agreements, whether explicit or implicit, can artificially inflate prices, restrict supply, and undermine the principles of fair competition. Market allocation is another prohibited practice where competitors divide markets among themselves, agreeing not to compete in specific geographic areas or segments. This behavior limits consumer choices and can lead to higher prices and reduced service quality, as firms no longer have to compete for business in their allocated territories. Both practices, price fixing and market allocation, not only distort the market but also erode trust in the real estate profession, potentially leading to severe legal penalties, including fines and imprisonment for individuals involved. Real estate professionals must also be wary of participating in group boycotts, another form of anti-competitive behavior. This occurs when several businesses collectively refuse to deal with a particular company or individual in an attempt to exclude them from the market. Such actions can unfairly limit competition and access to services, harming both consumers and the targeted entities. To ensure compliance with antitrust laws, real estate agents and brokers should focus on independent decision-making regarding pricing, marketing, and client interactions. They should avoid discussions of fees or business practices with competitors and should base all business decisions on their own strategies and the needs of their clients. Training and policies within real estate firms can help reinforce these principles, ensuring that all team members are aware of the boundaries set by antitrust laws.

Exercise:

What is the primary purpose of antitrust laws in real estate practice?

[A] To allow real estate professionals to set uniform service fees

[B] To encourage competition and protect consumer choices

[C] To enable market allocation agreements among competitors

[D] To restrict the number of real estate agents in a given area

Correct Answer: [B] To encourage competition and protect consumer choices

Explanation: The correct answer is B because the primary purpose of antitrust laws in the real estate industry, as in all industries, is to encourage fair competition and protect consumers from anti-competitive practices like price fixing, market allocation, and collusion. These laws ensure that consumers have access to a variety of choices and competitive prices. Options A, C, and D describe activities that are explicitly prohibited under antitrust laws, as they would limit competition and harm consumer interests.

CHAPTER 12: STATE-VARIED REAL ESTATE CALCULATIONS

Fundamentals of Real Estate Math

Math in Real Estate: Calculations and Costs

Calculating area is fundamental in real estate, especially when assessing the size of a property or land. The area is typically measured in square feet or acres in the United States. For rectangular or square properties, the area can be calculated by multiplying the length by the width. For example, a property that is 100 feet long and 50 feet wide has an area of 5,000 square feet. This calculation is crucial for determining the usable space, understanding zoning requirements, and evaluating property value. Determining property boundaries involves understanding the legal descriptions provided in property deeds. These descriptions often reference the lot and block system, metes and bounds, or the rectangular survey system. Basic math skills are necessary to interpret these descriptions and to calculate the precise location and dimensions of property boundaries. This ensures accuracy in property listings, aids in resolving disputes, and is essential for conducting land surveys.

Estimating property costs involves several mathematical calculations, including determining down payments, closing costs, property taxes, and insurance premiums. For instance, if a buyer is purchasing a home for $300,000 with a 20% down payment, the calculation would be $300,000 * 0.20 = $60,000. Additionally, understanding how to prorate taxes and calculate interest rates on mortgages requires the application of basic math principles. These calculations help buyers and sellers make informed financial decisions and plan for future expenses.

Exercise:

A property is listed as being 150 feet by 120 feet. What is the total area in square feet?

[A] 18,000 square feet

[B] 17,000 square feet

[C] 15,000 square feet

[D] 20,000 square feet

Correct Answer: [A] 18,000 square feet

Explanation: To find the area of the property, multiply the length by the width. In this case, 150 feet * 120 feet = 18,000 square feet. This calculation is a direct application of basic math to determine the size of a property, an essential step in evaluating its value and potential uses.

T-Bar Financial Analysis in Real Estate

The T-Bar Method of financial analysis is a visual tool that simplifies the understanding of financial transactions in real estate, particularly useful for calculating cash flows and investment returns. This method involves drawing a T-shaped figure where the top bar separates the inflows and outflows, and the vertical bar helps in balancing the two sides to determine the net result. On the left side of the T, you list all cash inflows, such as rental income, proceeds from a sale, or refinancing. On the right side, you record outflows, including purchase costs, renovation expenses, and operating costs. The goal is to balance both sides to see if the investment is profitable.

For real estate professionals, mastering the T-Bar Method is essential for evaluating the financial viability of properties and investment opportunities. It provides a clear, concise way to present and analyze the financial aspects of real estate transactions, making it easier to communicate with clients, lenders, and investors.

Exercise:

If a real estate investment has the following cash flows: $15,000 in rental income (inflow) and $5,000 in maintenance costs plus $2,000 in property taxes (outflows), what is the net cash flow using the T-Bar Method?

[A] $8,000 net inflow

[B] $7,000 net inflow

[C] $10,000 net inflow

[D] $12,000 net inflow

Correct Answer: [A] $8,000 net inflow

Explanation: Using the T-Bar Method, you would list the $15,000 rental income on the left side (inflows) and the sum of maintenance costs ($5,000) and property taxes ($2,000), totaling $7,000, on the right side (outflows). Subtracting the outflows from the inflows ($15,000 - $7,000) gives a net cash flow of $8,000, indicating a profitable investment. This calculation demonstrates the T-Bar Method's utility in visually organizing and analyzing the financial components of real estate transactions to determine their viability.

Real Estate Financial Calculations

Financial calculations in real estate transactions are critical for both buyers and sellers to understand as they navigate the complexities of purchasing, selling, and investing in property. These calculations include determining loan amounts, understanding how interest rates affect monthly payments, deciphering amortization schedules, and calculating return on investment (ROI) to assess the profitability of real estate investments. Loan amounts are typically determined by the purchase price of a property minus the down payment. The interest rate on a mortgage can significantly impact the total cost of a loan over time. Interest rates may be fixed, remaining constant over the life of the loan, or adjustable, changing at specified times. The choice between these types of rates affects not only the monthly payment but also the total interest paid over the life of the loan. Amortization schedules offer a detailed look at how each payment is divided between principal and interest over the life of the loan. Initially, a larger portion of each payment is applied toward interest, but as the loan balance decreases, more of each payment goes toward reducing the principal. Understanding an amortization schedule is crucial for real estate professionals as it helps in explaining to clients how long it will take to build equity in a property. Calculating the return on investment for real estate transactions involves analyzing the income and costs associated with a property to determine its profitability. ROI is calculated by dividing the net profit of the investment by the initial cost. For real estate, this could include rental income, appreciation, and tax benefits, minus expenses like mortgage payments, maintenance, and property taxes.

Exercise:

A buyer purchases a property for $300,000 with a down payment of $60,000. The buyer secures a 30-year fixed-rate mortgage at an annual interest rate of 4%. What is the monthly mortgage payment (principal and interest only)?

[A] $1,145.80

[B] $1,432.25

[C] $1,088.97

[D] $954.83

Correct Answer: [A] $1,145.80

Explanation: The loan amount would be the purchase price ($300,000) minus the down payment ($60,000), resulting in a loan amount of $240,000. Using the formula for calculating monthly mortgage payments or an online mortgage calculator, the monthly payment for a $240,000 loan at 4% interest over 30 years is approximately $1,145.80. This calculation does not include taxes, insurance, or other potential fees, focusing solely on principal and interest.

Understanding these financial calculations is essential for real estate professionals to guide their clients through the complexities of real estate transactions, ensuring informed decision-making and successful investments.

Mortgage, Tax, and Valuation Basics

Property taxes are a critical aspect of real estate ownership, calculated based on the assessed value of the property and the local tax rate. The formula for calculating property taxes is the assessed value of the property multiplied by the local tax rate. Understanding this calculation is essential for budgeting for annual property expenses and for advising clients on the long-term costs of owning a property.

Valuation techniques in real estate involve determining the value of a property using various methods, including the sales comparison approach, the cost approach, and the income approach. The sales comparison approach compares the property to similar properties that have recently sold, adjusting for differences. The cost approach estimates the cost to replace the property's structure, minus depreciation, plus the land value. The income approach is used for investment properties and is based on the income the property generates.

Exercise:

A property is assessed at a value of $250,000. The local property tax rate is 1.2%. What is the annual property tax?

[A] $2,500

[B] $3,000

[C] $2,000

[D] $3,000

Correct Answer: [B] $3,000

Explanation: The annual property tax is calculated by multiplying the assessed value of the property ($250,000) by the local tax rate (1.2%), which equals $3,000. This calculation is pivotal for understanding the annual expenses associated with property ownership and for setting realistic expectations for clients regarding the costs of owning real estate.

Valuation is a cornerstone of real estate practice, influencing decisions on pricing, investment, and taxation. Mastery of these calculations ensures real estate professionals can provide accurate, valuable advice to clients, supporting successful transactions and investment strategies.

Real Estate Depreciation Methods

Depreciation in real estate is a critical concept, allowing investors to account for the decrease in value of a property over time due to wear and tear, age, or obsolescence. Understanding how to calculate property value depreciation is essential for accurate financial analysis and tax planning. Two primary methods are used: straight-line depreciation and accelerated depreciation. Straight-line depreciation is the most straightforward method, dividing the cost of the property (excluding land) by its useful life, as determined by the IRS, to find the annual depreciation expense. For residential properties, the IRS has determined a useful life of 27.5 years, and for commercial properties, it's 39 years. This method spreads the cost evenly across the useful life of the property.

Accelerated depreciation, on the other hand, allows for a larger depreciation deduction in the early years of property ownership, with the amount decreasing over time. The Modified Accelerated Cost Recovery System (MACRS) is the current method allowed by the IRS for this purpose. MACRS uses a declining balance method, which can significantly reduce taxable income in the initial years following a property purchase. Both methods have a direct impact on property value and taxes. Depreciation reduces the property's book value on the balance sheet and decreases taxable income, thus affecting the property owner's tax liability. Real estate professionals must grasp these concepts to advise clients on investment strategies and tax implications effectively.

Exercise:

A residential rental property purchased for $275,000 (excluding land value) is being depreciated using the straight-line method. What is the annual depreciation expense, assuming a useful life of 27.5 years?

[A] $10,000

[B] $9,000

[C] $10,909.09

[D] $8,181.82

Correct Answer: [A] $10,000

Explanation: Using the straight-line method, the annual depreciation expense is calculated by dividing the property's cost by its useful life. Therefore, $275,000 divided by 27.5 years equals approximately $10,000 per year. This calculation demonstrates the straightforward approach of the straight-line method, providing a consistent annual depreciation expense that impacts the property's value and the owner's tax obligations over time.

Measuring Property Sizes and Boundaries

Measuring property sizes and boundaries accurately is crucial for real estate professionals, as these measurements affect legal documentation, sales listings, and valuation. Techniques and tools for measuring property vary based on the type of property and the precision required. For residential properties, square footage is a key metric, while acreage is more relevant for larger, undeveloped parcels of land. The use of a tape measure or laser distance measurer is common for determining the dimensions of rooms within a building, contributing to the total square footage calculation. This process involves measuring the length and width of each room and then multiplying these figures to get the area in square feet. For irregularly shaped rooms, the space may be divided into geometric shapes, with each section measured separately before summing the areas. For outdoor land measurements, particularly for large areas, more sophisticated tools like GPS devices, surveyor's wheels, or even drone technology may be employed to assess acreage accurately. These tools help in mapping property boundaries and calculating the total area, taking into account variations in terrain and any existing structures.

Legal descriptions of property, found in deeds and other real estate documents, often reference specific surveying methods such as metes and bounds, which describe boundaries in terms of landmarks and measurements, or the rectangular survey system, which divides land into a grid of townships and sections. Understanding these descriptions and being able to correlate them with physical measurements is essential for ensuring accuracy in property listings and transactions.

Exercise:

A real estate professional is measuring a rectangular plot of land using a surveyor's wheel. The length of the plot is measured as 150 feet and the width as 100 feet. What is the acreage of the plot?

[A] 0.34 acres

[B] 0.15 acres

[C] 1.5 acres

[D] 3.4 acres

Correct Answer: [A] 0.34 acres

Explanation: The acreage of the plot is calculated by multiplying the length by the width to get the total square footage, then converting that figure into acres. For this plot, 150 feet by 100 feet equals 15,000 square feet. Since one acre is equal to 43,560 square feet, dividing 15,000 by 43,560 gives approximately 0.34 acres. This calculation is fundamental for real estate professionals when assessing land size for listing and valuation purposes.

Applying Mathematical Concepts Through Examples

Exercise 1:

A real estate agent is listing a property that includes a main house and a detached garage. The main house is 2,500 square feet, and the detached garage is 500 square feet. If the agent wants to list the total square footage of the property, what should it be?

[A] 2,500 square feet

[B] 3,000 square feet

[C] 500 square feet

[D] 2,000 square feet

Correct Answer: [B] 3,000 square feet

Explanation: To find the total square footage of the property, add the square footage of the main house (2,500 square feet) to the square footage of the detached garage (500 square feet), which equals 3,000 square feet. This calculation is crucial for accurately listing properties, ensuring potential buyers have a clear understanding of the total available space.

Exercise 2:

A buyer is interested in a property listed at $350,000. They plan to make a down payment of 20%. How much will the down payment be?

[A] $70,000

[B] $35,000

[C] $7,000

[D] $280,000

Correct Answer: [A] $70,000

Explanation: The down payment is calculated as 20% of the purchase price. Therefore, 20% of $350,000 is $70,000. This calculation helps buyers understand the upfront costs associated with purchasing a property and is fundamental in planning financial commitments.

Exercise 3:

A property generates $24,000 in rental income annually. The operating expenses (maintenance, taxes, insurance) for the year total $6,000. What is the net operating income (NOI) of the

property?

[A] $18,000

[B] $30,000

[C] $6,000

[D] $24,000

Correct Answer: [A] $18,000

Explanation: The net operating income (NOI) is calculated by subtracting the total operating expenses from the total rental income. Therefore, $24,000 (rental income) - $6,000 (operating expenses) = $18,000. Understanding NOI is essential for evaluating the profitability of income-generating properties.

Exercise 4:

A real estate professional is calculating the commission for a property sold at $500,000 with a commission rate of 6%. What is the total commission?

[A] $30,000

[B] $3,000

[C] $300,000

[D] $60,000

Correct Answer: [A] $30,000

Explanation: The total commission is calculated by multiplying the sale price by the commission rate. Therefore, $500,000 * 6% = $30,000. This calculation is vital for real estate professionals to understand their earnings from transactions and for sellers to account for selling costs.

Exercise 5:

A client is looking at a mortgage with a principal of $200,000, an interest rate of 4% per annum, and a term of 30 years. What is the monthly mortgage payment (principal and interest only)?

[A] $954.83

[B] $1,432.25

[C] $1,088.97

[D] $666.67

Correct Answer: [A] $954.83

Explanation: Using the formula for calculating monthly mortgage payments or an online mortgage calculator, the monthly payment for a $200,000 loan at 4% interest over 30 years is approximately $954.83. This calculation does not include taxes, insurance, or other potential fees, focusing solely on principal and interest, and is crucial for buyers to understand their monthly financial commitments when purchasing a property.

CHAPTER 13: FAIR HOUSING AND ETHICAL PRACTICES

Fair Housing Laws: Key Provisions and Obligations

The Fair Housing Act, enacted in 1968 and amended over the years, stands as a pivotal piece of legislation designed to eliminate discrimination in housing based on race, color, national origin, religion, sex, familial status, or disability. This act applies to a wide range of housing-related activities, including renting or buying a home, getting a mortgage, seeking housing assistance, or engaging in other housing-related transactions. Real estate professionals must understand that the act prohibits practices such as refusing to sell or rent a dwelling to someone from a protected class, making housing unavailable, setting different terms or conditions for sale or rental, and providing different housing services or facilities. Additionally, the act extends to advertising by prohibiting the publication of any notice or advertisement indicating a preference, limitation, or discrimination based on these protected classes. This ensures that all listings and marketing materials used by real estate professionals are crafted in a manner that promotes inclusivity and fairness. State and local regulations may introduce additional protected classes beyond those covered by the Fair Housing Act. These can include protections based on sexual orientation, gender identity, source of income, and marital status, among others. Real estate professionals must familiarize themselves with these laws as they vary significantly across different jurisdictions. Ignorance of local laws is not a defense against discrimination claims, making it imperative for professionals to conduct due diligence and ensure compliance with both federal and local regulations. The legal obligations of real estate professionals under the Fair Housing Act and other anti-discrimination laws are profound. They are required to treat all clients equally, providing the same level of service and access to all available properties that meet the client's criteria, regardless of their membership in a protected class. This includes showing properties in diverse neighborhoods and avoiding the illegal practice of steering, where agents might guide clients towards or away from certain areas based on discriminatory reasons.

Exercise:

Which of the following actions is prohibited under the Fair Housing Act?

[A] Refusing to rent an apartment to a person because of their religion

[B] Publishing a property advertisement stating "Ideal for singles"

[C] Offering a discount to a tenant who refers a friend

[D] All of the above

Correct Answer: [D] All of the above

Explanation: The Fair Housing Act prohibits discrimination based on race, color, national origin, religion, sex, familial status, or disability. This includes refusing to rent or sell to someone because of their religion (A), making discriminatory statements in advertisements (B), and suggesting a preference for certain types of tenants in a way that could discourage or exclude others based on protected characteristics (B). Offering a discount for referrals is not inherently discriminatory unless it is applied in a manner that excludes or disadvantages people from protected classes. However, as described, both A and B are clear violations of the act, making D the correct answer as it encompasses all listed prohibited actions. Enforcement of the Fair Housing Act and related state and local regulations is carried out by the Department of Housing and Urban Development (HUD). When a complaint of housing discrimination is filed, HUD investigates the allegation and can take legal action against violators. Penalties for non-compliance can include fines, damages awarded to victims, and mandatory corrective actions such as training and policy changes for the offending party. Real estate professionals must therefore not only understand the laws but also implement practices and policies that ensure compliance to avoid legal repercussions. Training and education play a critical role in preventing discrimination and promoting fair housing practices. Many real estate firms and associations offer training programs designed to help agents understand their obligations under the law and how to conduct their business in a way that is fair and equitable for all clients. Participation in these programs not only helps in compliance but also enhances the professionalism and reputation of real estate practitioners.

Real estate professionals are also advised to develop and follow a standard operating procedure (SOP) that outlines how to handle all aspects of the housing transaction process in a manner that complies with fair housing laws. This includes procedures for advertising, showing properties, application processing, and client interactions. Having such procedures in place not only helps in ensuring compliance but also serves as a defense in case of a discrimination claim.

Exercise:

What is the role of the Department of Housing and Urban Development (HUD) in enforcing the Fair Housing Act?

[A] To provide financial assistance to homebuyers

[B] To investigate complaints of housing discrimination

[C] To set interest rates for mortgages

[D] To build affordable housing

Correct Answer: [B] To investigate complaints of housing discrimination

Explanation: HUD's primary role in enforcing the Fair Housing Act is to investigate complaints of housing discrimination. When a complaint is filed, HUD examines the allegations and determines whether there is reasonable cause to believe discrimination occurred. If discrimination is found, HUD can take legal action against the violators, including imposing penalties and requiring corrective measures. This enforcement mechanism is crucial in upholding the principles of the Fair Housing Act and ensuring that housing opportunities are made available to all individuals on an equal basis.

Real estate professionals must remain vigilant and proactive in their efforts to support fair housing. This includes staying informed about changes in laws and regulations, participating in ongoing education on fair housing practices, and fostering an inclusive environment that welcomes diversity. By doing so, they not only comply with legal requirements but also contribute to a more equitable and just housing market. In conclusion, the Fair Housing Act and other anti-discrimination laws establish a legal framework that promotes equality in housing. Real estate professionals play a vital role in implementing these laws, requiring a commitment to ethical practices, continuous education, and a proactive approach to compliance. Through such efforts, the real estate industry can help ensure that housing opportunities are accessible to all, free from discrimination.

Ethical Real Estate Practices: Honesty and Integrity

Ethical conduct in real estate transcends mere compliance with legal standards; it embodies the principles of honesty, transparency, and integrity, ensuring that professionals act in the best interests of their clients while fostering trust and confidence in the real estate profession. The National Association of Realtors' (NAR) Code of Ethics stands as a cornerstone for ethical behavior, setting forth the duties and responsibilities real estate professionals owe to clients, the public, and other real estate professionals. This Code emphasizes the importance of conducting business with the highest level of integrity and ethical consideration, ensuring that all actions taken are in compliance with both the spirit and the letter of the law. The Code of Ethics is divided into three main areas: Duties to Clients and Customers, Duties to the Public, and Duties to Realtors. Each section outlines specific obligations designed to guide real estate professionals in their daily interactions and decision-making processes. For instance, the duty to treat all clients with honesty implies that real estate professionals must not mislead or withhold information about the property or transaction, regardless of the potential impact on the sale. Transparency in real estate transactions is crucial, requiring the full disclosure of any conflicts of interest, property defects, or other material facts that could influence a client's decision.

Integrity in real estate practice means adhering to a set of moral and ethical principles, ensuring fairness and honesty in all transactions. This includes respecting the confidentiality of client information, avoiding exaggeration and misrepresentation, and ensuring that all advertising and representations are truthful and not misleading. Real estate professionals are also expected to uphold the dignity of their profession, avoiding any conduct that could bring discredit to the real estate industry or the professional association they represent.

Exercise:

According to the National Association of Realtors' Code of Ethics, which of the following actions is required of real estate professionals?

[A] Disclosing only the information about a property that is beneficial to the seller

[B] Providing equal professional services to all clients, regardless of race, color, religion, sex, handicap, familial status, national origin, sexual orientation, or gender identity

[C] Using advertising that promises more than what is realistically deliverable to attract clients

[D] Sharing confidential client information with other parties if it increases the likelihood of a transaction closing

Correct Answer: [B] Providing equal professional services to all clients, regardless of race, color, religion, sex, handicap, familial status, national origin, sexual orientation, or gender identity

Explanation: The correct answer is [B] because the National Association of Realtors' Code of Ethics emphasizes the importance of providing equal professional services to all clients, ensuring that there is no discrimination in the provision of real estate services. This commitment to equality and fairness is a fundamental ethical obligation, reflecting the industry's dedication to upholding the highest standards of integrity and professionalism. Options [A], [C], and [D] are contrary to the ethical standards set forth in the Code, as they involve misleading actions, false advertising, and breach of confidentiality, all of which are unethical practices in the real estate profession.

By adhering to the ethical standards outlined in the National Association of Realtors' Code of Ethics, real estate professionals not only ensure compliance with legal requirements but also contribute to a culture of trust and respect within the industry and among the public. Ethical conduct is not just about avoiding wrongdoing; it is about actively doing right by all parties involved in a real estate transaction, thereby elevating the profession and ensuring its continued respect and credibility.

Handling Real Estate Discrimination Complaints

When a discrimination complaint arises in real estate transactions, it triggers a specific set of procedures aimed at addressing and resolving the issue. These procedures are critical for maintaining fairness and integrity within the housing market, ensuring that all individuals have equal access to housing opportunities without facing discrimination. Real estate professionals play a significant role in this process, from the initial handling of complaints to the resolution phase. Upon receiving a discrimination complaint, the first step for a real estate professional is to document the complaint thoroughly. This includes recording the details of the incident, the parties involved, and any witnesses or evidence that could support the investigation. It's imperative for real estate professionals to understand that their role is not to judge or dismiss the complaint but to ensure it is directed to the appropriate authority for investigation. The complaint is then reported to the relevant state or federal agency. In the United States, the Department of Housing and Urban Development (HUD) is the federal agency responsible for investigating housing discrimination complaints under the Fair Housing Act. State and local fair housing agencies also investigate complaints and work in partnership with HUD. Real estate professionals must be familiar with the reporting procedures of these agencies and may be required to assist their clients in filing a complaint. Once a complaint is filed, the agency will conduct an investigation. This process involves gathering evidence, interviewing the complainant, the respondent (the party the complaint is filed against), and any witnesses. Real estate professionals may be called upon to provide information or evidence as part of this investigation. It's crucial for professionals to cooperate fully with the investigation, providing accurate and complete information to the investigating agency.

If the investigation finds evidence of discrimination, the agency may attempt to resolve the complaint through conciliation—a voluntary agreement between the complainant and the respondent to address the issues raised in the complaint. Real estate professionals may play a role in facilitating these discussions or agreements, ensuring that any resolution complies with fair housing laws.

Should conciliation fail or if discrimination is found and not adequately addressed, legal action may be taken against the respondent. Penalties for violating fair housing laws can include fines, damages to the complainant for harm caused by the discrimination, and orders to take corrective actions, such as training or policy changes. Real estate professionals involved in or associated with the discriminatory practice may also face penalties, including fines, suspension, or revocation of their license, and mandatory participation in fair housing training.

Exercise:

What is the first step a real estate professional should take upon receiving a discrimination complaint?

[A] Dismiss the complaint if it seems unfounded

[B] Document the complaint thoroughly

[C] Advise the complainant to forget about the incident

[D] Immediately take legal action against the accused party

Correct Answer: [B] Document the complaint thoroughly

Explanation: The correct first step is to document the complaint thoroughly. This involves recording all relevant details of the alleged discrimination, including what happened, who was involved, and any evidence that may support the claim. This documentation is crucial for ensuring that the complaint is addressed appropriately and is a necessary step before reporting the incident to the appropriate investigating agency. Options [A], [C], and [D] are not appropriate actions for a real estate professional to take upon receiving a discrimination complaint, as they do not align with the procedural and ethical standards set forth by fair housing laws and regulations.

Handling discrimination complaints with diligence, respect, and in accordance with the law not only helps protect the rights of individuals but also upholds the integrity of the real estate profession. Real estate professionals must be knowledgeable about fair housing laws, understand the complaint process, and be prepared to play their part in ensuring compliance and addressing issues of discrimination in the housing market.

Ethics and Law in Real Estate

Fair Housing Laws and Ethical Standards are intertwined, reflecting the core values of integrity, equality, and justice in real estate practice. These laws, established to prevent discrimination and promote inclusivity in housing, are not only legal obligations but also moral imperatives that guide the professional conduct of real estate agents. Upholding these laws goes beyond mere compliance; it embodies a commitment to ethical responsibility, ensuring that every individual has equal access to housing opportunities without bias or prejudice. The ethical standards in real estate practice demand that professionals treat all clients with fairness and respect, regardless of their race, color, religion, sex, disability, familial status, or national origin. This commitment to ethical practice reinforces the legal requirements set forth by the Fair Housing Act and other anti-discrimination laws, creating a professional environment that respects the dignity and rights of all individuals. Real estate agents are expected to conduct their business in a way that promotes the principles of fairness and equality, demonstrating a clear understanding of both the letter and the spirit of fair housing laws.

Exercise:

What is the primary ethical responsibility of real estate professionals under fair housing laws?

[A] To maximize profits for their agency

[B] To ensure all marketing materials specify preferred client demographics

[C] To provide equal professional services to all individuals, regardless of protected characteristics

[D] To only show properties in certain neighborhoods to maintain property values

Correct Answer: [C] To provide equal professional services to all individuals, regardless of protected characteristics

Explanation: The primary ethical responsibility under fair housing laws is to provide equal professional services to all individuals, regardless of protected characteristics (C). This responsibility is fundamental to ethical real estate practice, ensuring that every person has equal access to housing opportunities. Options [A], [B], and [D] are not only unethical but also illegal under fair housing laws, as they promote discriminatory practices and undermine the principles of equality and justice that form the foundation of the real estate profession. Adherence to fair housing laws and ethical standards is crucial for maintaining the integrity of the real estate profession. It fosters trust among clients and the public, enhancing the reputation of real estate professionals as champions of fairness and equality. By committing to these ethical practices, real estate agents not only fulfill their legal obligations but also contribute to a more equitable and inclusive society. This commitment to ethical responsibility and professional conduct is what distinguishes the real estate profession, ensuring that it remains a respected and trusted field for generations to come.

CHAPTER 14: TEST PREP AND STRATEGIES

Effective Study Techniques for Exam Success

Effective study techniques are paramount for aspiring real estate agents aiming to excel in their licensing exam. Among these, spaced repetition, active recall, and the utilization of practice exams stand out as particularly effective methods for cementing knowledge and enhancing recall capabilities. Spaced repetition involves reviewing study material at increasing intervals over time, which has been shown to significantly improve memory retention. This method leverages the psychological spacing effect, ensuring that information is revisited just as it begins to fade from memory, thereby strengthening the learning process. Active recall, on the other hand, requires actively stimulating memory during the learning process. Instead of passively reading or highlighting text, students are encouraged to test themselves on the material, either through flashcards, practice questions, or teaching the content to someone else. This technique forces the brain to retrieve information, thereby making the memory stronger and more likely to be recalled in the future. The use of practice exams serves multiple purposes. Firstly, it familiarizes candidates with the format and structure of the actual exam, reducing anxiety and improving time management skills. Secondly, it identifies areas of strength and weakness, allowing for targeted study in areas that require further understanding. Practice exams also simulate the pressure of the real test environment, helping students to develop resilience and strategies for managing stress and fatigue. Organizing study materials and creating a study schedule are equally critical to exam preparation success. A well-organized study plan ensures that all necessary material is covered, with sufficient time allocated to each topic. It also prevents last-minute cramming, which is less effective and more stressful. A study schedule should be realistic, allowing for breaks and flexibility to adjust as needed based on progress and comprehension. It should also include specific goals for each study session, ensuring that time is used efficiently and effectively.

Incorporating these study techniques into a comprehensive exam preparation strategy can significantly increase the likelihood of passing the real estate licensing exam. By understanding and applying these methods, candidates can optimize their study time, improve retention, and enhance their overall test performance, setting a strong foundation for a successful career in real estate.

Test Anxiety: Management and Strategies

Managing test anxiety and stress effectively is crucial for maximizing performance on the real estate licensing exam. Strategies to combat these challenges include adopting relaxation techniques, ensuring adequate sleep, maintaining a nutritious diet, and fostering a positive mindset. Each of these components plays a vital role in preparing both the mind and body for the rigors of test-taking. Relaxation techniques such as deep breathing exercises, meditation, and progressive muscle relaxation can significantly reduce physical and mental stress. These practices help in calming nerves, improving concentration, and enhancing the ability to recall information under pressure. Implementing these techniques into daily study routines can make them more effective when applied just before or during the exam. Adequate sleep is another cornerstone of managing test anxiety. Sleep plays a critical role in memory consolidation, problem-solving abilities, and cognitive function. Aspiring real estate agents should aim for 7-9 hours of quality sleep per night, especially in the days leading up to the exam. Establishing a regular sleep schedule helps regulate the body's internal clock, leading to improved sleep quality and mental alertness. Nutrition also impacts cognitive function and emotional well-being. A diet rich in fruits, vegetables, whole grains, lean proteins, and omega-3 fatty acids can enhance brain health and mood. Avoiding excessive caffeine and sugar before the exam can prevent spikes and crashes in energy levels, helping maintain steady focus throughout the test.

Cultivating a positive mindset is equally important. Confidence and a positive attitude towards the exam are fostered by thorough preparation, understanding of the material, and realistic practice through mock exams. Setting realistic goals, celebrating small achievements during the study process, and maintaining a supportive network of peers or mentors can also bolster confidence and reduce anxiety.

Implementing these strategies requires discipline and commitment but can significantly improve the ability to manage test anxiety and stress. By taking care of their physical and mental health, candidates can approach the real estate licensing exam with confidence, clarity, and the resilience needed to perform at their best.

Effective Exam Strategies and Tips

Reading directions carefully is the first step to ensuring that you fully understand what is being asked before you attempt to answer a question. This might seem straightforward, yet under the pressure of an exam, many candidates rush through instructions, leading to avoidable mistakes. Take a moment to read through each question and its directions thoroughly, even if it means reading them twice. This ensures that you grasp the specifics of what the examiners are looking for, whether it's selecting one correct answer or multiple correct responses. Managing time during the test is critical. Before starting, quickly scan through the exam to gauge the length and complexity of the questions. This will help you allocate your time wisely, spending more time on sections that carry more weight or are more challenging, and less time on those that are simpler or more straightforward. A common strategy is to answer the questions you know first, then return to tackle the more difficult ones, ensuring that you're not leaving any easy points on the table due to a time crunch. Using the process of elimination on multiple-choice questions can significantly increase your chances of selecting the correct answer, even when you're unsure. By systematically ruling out the options you know are incorrect, you narrow down the possible correct answers, increasing the probability of choosing the right one. This technique also helps you focus on the details of the remaining options, which might give you further clues to the correct answer.

Reviewing answers thoroughly before submitting your exam is an essential final step. If time permits, go back to the questions you were uncertain about or that you flagged for review. Read the question and your answer again, checking for any mistakes in your reasoning or errors you might have made in haste. This is also the time to ensure that you've answered every question, as an unanswered question is a guaranteed zero.

Exercise:

What is the most effective strategy for managing time during a multiple-choice exam?

[A] Answer the questions in order, regardless of difficulty

[B] Spend equal time on each question

[C] Start with the hardest questions to ensure they get done

[D] Answer easy questions first, then return to more difficult ones

Correct Answer: [D] Answer easy questions first, then return to more difficult ones

Explanation: Starting with the easier questions allows you to secure all the points you confidently can while ensuring you're not wasting precious time on harder questions that might take longer to answer. This strategy not only maximizes your score but also helps manage exam time effectively, giving you the opportunity to return to and spend more time on the questions that require more thought.

CHAPTER 15: PRACTICE EXAMS

Chapter 1: Real Estate Exam Prep

Question 1: Which of the following best describes the concept of "bundle of rights" in real estate?

[A] The legal restrictions placed on property by governmental entities

[B] The rights of tenants when leasing a property

[C] The collection of legal rights associated with the ownership of property

[D] The responsibilities of a property owner to the local community

Correct Answer: [C] The collection of legal rights associated with the ownership of property

Explanation: The "bundle of rights" is a term used in real estate to describe the set of legal rights conferred to the property owner. These rights include the right to possess, control, enjoy, exclude others, and dispose of the property. This concept is fundamental in understanding property ownership and the legal implications that come with it.

Question 2: What is the primary difference between real property and personal property?

[A] Real property includes movable items, while personal property includes immovable items

[B] Real property is always more valuable than personal property

[C] Real property includes land and anything attached to it, while personal property includes movable items

[D] There is no significant difference between the two

Correct Answer: [C] Real property includes land and anything attached to it, while personal property includes movable items

Explanation: Real property refers to land and any permanent structures or improvements attached to it, such as buildings or trees. Personal property, on the other hand, consists of movable items that are not permanently affixed to the land, such as furniture or vehicles. Understanding this distinction is crucial for real estate transactions and legal processes.

Question 3: Which of the following best defines a joint tenancy?

[A] Ownership by one individual

[B] Ownership by two or more parties who do not have survivorship rights

[C] Ownership by two or more parties with equal interest and survivorship rights

[D] A form of lease agreement between tenants

Correct Answer: [C] Ownership by two or more parties with equal interest and survivorship rights

Explanation: Joint tenancy is a form of co-ownership where two or more individuals own property together, each with an equal share and with survivorship rights. This means that upon the death of one joint tenant, their interest in the property automatically passes to the surviving joint tenant(s), rather than being part of the deceased's estate.

Question 4: What does the term "market value" refer to in real estate?

[A] The highest price a property would sell for in a competitive auction

[B] The price set by the local government for tax purposes

[C] The most probable price a property should bring in a fair sale

[D] The price a property is listed for on the market

Correct Answer: [C] The most probable price a property should bring in a fair sale

Explanation: Market value in real estate is defined as the most probable price a property would command in a competitive and open market under all conditions requisite to a fair sale. This assumes that the buyer and seller are each acting prudently, knowledgeably, and that the price is not affected by undue stimulus.

Question 5: Which of the following is NOT a method of legal description of property?

[A] Metes and Bounds

[B] Rectangular Survey System

[C] Lot and Block

[D] Color-coded Maps

Correct Answer: [D] Color-coded Maps

Explanation: Legal descriptions of property are specific ways to define and describe the location and boundaries of a property for legal transactions. The primary methods include Metes and Bounds, Rectangular Survey System, and Lot and Block. Color-coded maps, while useful for visual representation, are not a legally recognized method for describing property boundaries and locations.

Practice Exam 2: Property Ownership and Land Use

Question 1: Which zoning classification permits the operation of manufacturing facilities?

[A] Residential

[B] Commercial

[C] Industrial

[D] Agricultural

Correct Answer: [C] Industrial

Explanation: Industrial zoning is designated for areas involved in manufacturing, production, and distribution of goods. Facilities such as factories and warehouses are typically found in these zones. Residential, commercial, and agricultural zones have different purposes, focusing on living spaces, business operations, and farming activities, respectively.

Question 2: What is the primary purpose of a variance in land use?

[A] To change the zoning laws of a city

[B] To allow a deviation from current zoning requirements for a specific property

[C] To increase the density of residential units allowed

[D] To decrease property taxes

Correct Answer: [B] To allow a deviation from current zoning requirements for a specific property

Explanation: A variance is a legal mechanism that allows property owners to deviate from strict adherence to current zoning requirements. It is typically sought when a property cannot be feasibly used under the current zoning regulations, allowing for exceptions without needing to change the zoning laws for the entire area.

Question 3: Which type of deed provides the greatest protection to the buyer?

[A] Quitclaim deed

[B] Warranty deed

[C] Special warranty deed

[D] Grant deed

Correct Answer: [B] Warranty deed

Explanation: A warranty deed offers the highest level of protection for the buyer, as it guarantees that the seller holds clear title to the property and has the right to sell it. It also assures the buyer of compensation in case any claims against the property arise after the sale. Quitclaim, special warranty, and grant deeds offer varying levels of protection, with the quitclaim deed offering the least.

Question 4: What is an easement?

[A] A right to use the property of another for a specific purpose

[B] A restriction on the use of property imposed by a previous owner

[C] A government action transferring private property to public use

[D] A temporary lease of property rights

Correct Answer: [A] A right to use the property of another for a specific purpose

Explanation: An easement is a legal right granted to a non-owner to use the property for a specific purpose, such as access to a road or utility lines. It does not confer ownership but allows limited use or access, which is typically recorded with the property deed.

Question 5: What does the principle of eminent domain allow?

[A] Private entities to purchase property without consent

[B] Homeowners to sell their property directly to the government

[C] The government to take private property for public use, with compensation

[D] The transfer of property rights without compensation

Correct Answer: [C] The government to take private property for public use, with compensation

Explanation: Eminent domain is a legal principle that allows the government to take private property for public use, provided the owner is given just compensation. This process is used for projects that benefit the public, such as roads, parks, and schools. It is a constitutional right under the Fifth Amendment, which requires the provision of fair compensation to the affected property owner.

Question 6: Which term describes the legal process by which a tenant's right to occupy a property is terminated due to a breach of the lease agreement?

[A] Foreclosure

[B] Eviction

[C] Condemnation

[D] Repossession

Correct Answer: [B] Eviction

Explanation: Eviction is the legal process by which a landlord may terminate a tenant's right to occupy the premises due to a breach of the lease agreement, such as non-payment of rent or violating lease terms. The process is governed by state law and typically requires the landlord to provide notice and obtain a court order.

Question 7: What is the primary difference between a general warranty deed and a special warranty deed?

[A] A general warranty deed guarantees the property's title against all defects, whereas a special warranty deed only covers the period during which the seller owned the property

[B] A special warranty deed offers more protection to the buyer than a general warranty deed

[C] A general warranty deed is used for commercial properties, while a special warranty deed is used for residential properties

[D] There is no significant difference between the two

Correct Answer: [A] A general warranty deed guarantees the property's title against all defects, whereas a special warranty deed only covers the period during which the seller owned the property

Explanation: The key difference between these two types of deeds lies in the scope of the warranty provided by the seller. A general warranty deed offers broad protection, covering all title defects, even those that arose before the seller's ownership. In contrast, a special warranty deed limits protection to issues that occurred during the seller's period of ownership, offering less comprehensive coverage to the buyer.

Practice Exam 3: Valuation and Market Analysis

Question 1: Which appraisal method is most commonly used in the valuation of residential real estate?

[A] Cost approach

[B] Sales comparison approach

[C] Income approach

[D] Capitalization rate

Correct Answer: [B] Sales comparison approach

Explanation: The sales comparison approach is the most commonly used method in the valuation of residential real estate. It involves comparing the subject property with similar properties that have recently sold in the same area, adjusting for differences to determine the property's market value. This method is preferred for residential properties due to the availability of comparable sales data.

Question 2: What does the principle of highest and best use imply in real estate valuation?

[A] The current use of the property is always the most valuable

[B] The property's value is maximized when its use is most profitable and legally permissible

[C] The best use of a property is determined by its zoning classification

[D] Properties should be used in ways that are environmentally sustainable

Correct Answer: [B] The property's value is maximized when its use is most profitable and legally permissible

Explanation: The principle of highest and best use states that a property's value is maximized when its use is the most profitable and legally permissible. This concept is crucial in real estate valuation, as it considers not just the current use but the potential uses that could yield the highest return, within the bounds of what is legally allowed.

Question 3: Which factor is NOT directly considered in the income approach to property valuation?

[A] Net operating income

[B] Capitalization rate

[C] Color of the property

[D] Annual gross rental income

Correct Answer: [C] Color of the property

Explanation: The income approach to property valuation focuses on the income-producing potential of the property. It considers factors such as net operating income, capitalization rate, and annual gross rental income to determine value. The color of the property is not a factor in this valuation method, as it does not directly affect the property's ability to generate income.

Question 4: In market analysis, what role does demographic analysis play?

[A] It predicts the future value of properties based on past sales

[B] It assesses the impact of environmental regulations on property values

[C] It helps understand the potential demand for real estate in an area based on population characteristics

[D] It determines the legal restrictions on property use

Correct Answer: [C] It helps understand the potential demand for real estate in an area based on population characteristics

Explanation: Demographic analysis in market analysis plays a crucial role in understanding the potential demand for real estate in an area. By examining population characteristics such as age, income, family size, and growth trends, real estate professionals can predict which types of properties will be in demand and plan developments accordingly. This analysis is fundamental in making informed investment and development decisions.

Question 5: What is the significance of a comparative market analysis (CMA) in real estate?

[A] It determines the cost to build a replica of the subject property

[B] It provides a legal framework for zoning disputes

[C] It assesses the environmental impact of a property

[D] It estimates a property's market value by comparing it to similar properties that have sold, are listed, or failed to sell

Correct Answer: [D] It estimates a property's market value by comparing it to similar properties that have sold, are listed, or failed to sell

Explanation: A comparative market analysis (CMA) is a tool used in real estate to estimate a property's market value. It involves comparing the subject property to similar properties in the same area that have recently sold, are currently listed, or failed to sell. This comparison helps in determining a competitive market price for the property, making it a critical step in the listing or buying process.

Question 6: Which of the following best describes the term "market trends" in real estate?

[A] The architectural styles that are popular in a specific area

[B] The fluctuation of property taxes over time

[C] The patterns and movements in real estate prices over a period

[D] The legal changes affecting property ownership

Correct Answer: [C] The patterns and movements in real estate prices over a period

Explanation: Market trends in real estate refer to the patterns and movements in real estate prices over a period. These trends can indicate the direction in which the market is moving, such as whether it's a buyer's or seller's market, and help predict future price movements. Understanding market trends is essential for investors, real estate professionals, and buyers or sellers to make informed decisions.

Question 7: What is the primary purpose of conducting a market analysis in real estate?

[A] To fulfill legal requirements for property transactions

[B] To determine the best color for painting a property before sale

[C] To understand the current conditions and potential future trends in the real estate market

[D] To calculate the exact square footage of a property

Correct Answer: [C] To understand the current conditions and potential future trends in the real estate market

Explanation: The primary purpose of conducting a market analysis in real estate is to understand the current conditions and potential future trends in the market. This analysis provides valuable insights into factors such as demand, supply, pricing trends, and economic indicators that affect the real estate market. It helps stakeholders make informed decisions regarding buying, selling, investing, or developing properties.

Practice Exam 4: Real Estate Financing

Question 1: What is the primary advantage of a fixed-rate mortgage for a borrower?

[A] The interest rate can decrease over time

[B] The monthly payments remain the same throughout the life of the loan

[C] It offers lower interest rates than adjustable-rate mortgages

[D] It does not require a down payment

Correct Answer: [B] The monthly payments remain the same throughout the life of the loan

Explanation: A fixed-rate mortgage locks in the interest rate for the entire term of the loan, which means the monthly principal and interest payments remain constant. This predictability is a significant advantage for borrowers who prefer stable payments that won't change with market fluctuations.

Question 2: What does the term "amortization" refer to in real estate financing?

[A] The process of decreasing property values over time

[B] The division of a mortgage payment into parts that go toward principal and interest

[C] The increase in property value due to improvements

[D] The calculation of adjustable mortgage rates

Correct Answer: [B] The division of a mortgage payment into parts that go toward principal and interest

Explanation: Amortization in real estate financing refers to the process of spreading out a loan into a series of fixed payments over time. Each payment is divided into two parts: one part goes toward paying the loan's interest, and the other part goes toward reducing the loan's principal balance.

Question 3: Which type of loan is specifically designed to assist first-time homebuyers with a low down payment requirement?

[A] Conventional loan

[B] FHA loan

[C] VA loan

[D] Adjustable-rate mortgage

Correct Answer: [B] FHA loan

Explanation: FHA loans are insured by the Federal Housing Administration and are designed to help first-time homebuyers and those with low to moderate incomes. They require lower minimum down payments and credit scores than many conventional loans, making homeownership more accessible.

Question 4: What factor primarily influences the interest rate that a borrower will pay on a mortgage loan?

[A] The borrower's credit score

[B] The size of the property being purchased

[C] The current state of the economy

[D] The loan-to-value ratio

Correct Answer: [A] The borrower's credit score

Explanation: A borrower's credit score is a critical factor that lenders use to determine the interest rate on a mortgage loan. Higher credit scores generally result in lower interest rates because they indicate to lenders that the borrower has a history of managing credit responsibly.

Question 5: What is the purpose of a title search in the mortgage process?

[A] To determine the property's market value

[B] To verify the borrower's credit history

[C] To ensure the property is free from liens or other encumbrances

[D] To calculate the property's tax rate

Correct Answer: [C] To ensure the property is free from liens or other encumbrances

Explanation: A title search is conducted during the mortgage process to verify the seller's right to transfer ownership and to ensure the property is free from any liens, encumbrances, or claims. This is crucial for protecting the buyer and lender's interests in the property.

Question 6: Which statement best describes a balloon mortgage?

[A] It offers borrowers lower interest rates in exchange for a larger down payment

[B] It requires borrowers to make small payments for a set period, followed by a large payment to pay off the loan balance

[C] It automatically adjusts the interest rate based on market conditions

[D] It is a 30-year fixed-rate mortgage that is the standard in the industry

Correct Answer: [B] It requires borrowers to make small payments for a set period, followed by a large payment to pay off the loan balance

Explanation: A balloon mortgage requires borrowers to make relatively small monthly payments for a set period, typically 5 to 7 years, followed by a large "balloon" payment that pays off the remaining balance of the loan. This type of mortgage can be risky for borrowers who may not have the funds available to make the large final payment.

Question 7: What is the primary benefit of obtaining a pre-approval for a mortgage loan?

[A] It locks in an interest rate for the borrower

[B] It guarantees that the borrower will receive the loan amount stated in the pre-approval

[C] It gives the borrower an idea of how much they can afford when house hunting

[D] It eliminates the need for a down payment

Correct Answer: [C] It gives the borrower an idea of how much they can afford when house hunting

Explanation: Obtaining a pre-approval for a mortgage loan provides borrowers with an estimate of how much they can afford to borrow based on their financial situation. This helps in narrowing down the search for a home to those within the borrower's budget, making the house-hunting process more efficient.

Practice Exam 5: Agency Law and Contracts

Question 1: Which of the following best describes the fiduciary duty of loyalty in a real estate agency relationship?

[A] The agent's obligation to work in the best interest of the seller only

[B] The agent's responsibility to secure the highest possible price for the buyer

[C] The agent's duty to act in the best interests of the principal

[D] The agent's commitment to avoid dual agency scenarios

Correct Answer: [C] The agent's duty to act in the best interests of the principal

Explanation: The fiduciary duty of loyalty requires an agent to act at all times in the best interests of the principal, not the interests of the agent or any third party. This duty is fundamental in ensuring that the agent's actions are aligned with the principal's goals and objectives, whether representing a buyer or a seller in a real estate transaction.

Question 2: What is the primary purpose of a listing agreement in a real estate transaction?

[A] To outline the terms under which a property is leased to a tenant

[B] To document the commission structure for a mortgage broker

[C] To establish the contractual relationship between a seller and their agent

[D] To define the closing costs associated with a real estate transaction

Correct Answer: [C] To establish the contractual relationship between a seller and their agent

Explanation: A listing agreement is a contract between a seller and a real estate agent or broker that outlines the terms under which the agent will sell the property. This includes details such as the duration of the agreement, the listing price, and the commission structure. It formally establishes the agency relationship, allowing the agent to act on behalf of the seller.

Question 3: Which of the following is a characteristic of an exclusive right-to-sell listing agreement?

[A] The seller can sell the property themselves without paying a commission

[B] The property can be listed with multiple brokers simultaneously

[C] Only the listing broker is entitled to a commission if the property sells during the listing period

[D] The seller must pay a commission to the listing broker only if the broker sells the property

Correct Answer: [C] Only the listing broker is entitled to a commission if the property sells during the listing period

Explanation: An exclusive right-to-sell listing agreement gives the listing broker the exclusive right to earn a commission by acting as the agent for the seller and bringing a buyer. If the property sells during the term of the agreement, the listing broker is entitled to a commission, regardless of who actually finds the buyer.

Question 4: What is the primary legal effect of a contract that lacks consideration?

[A] The contract is still enforceable if both parties agree to it verbally

[B] The contract is considered voidable at the option of the seller

[C] The contract is generally considered unenforceable due to lack of consideration

[D] The contract automatically becomes a lease agreement

Correct Answer: [C] The contract is generally considered unenforceable due to lack of consideration

Explanation: Consideration is a legal term that refers to something of value that is exchanged between the parties in a contract. Without consideration, a contract lacks one of the essential elements required for it to be legally binding and enforceable. Therefore, a contract without consideration is generally considered unenforceable.

Question 5: In a real estate transaction, what is the purpose of an earnest money deposit?

[A] To cover the closing costs associated with the transaction

[B] To serve as the buyer's initial payment toward the purchase price

[C] To compensate the real estate agents for their services

[D] To demonstrate the buyer's serious intent to purchase the property

Correct Answer: [D] To demonstrate the buyer's serious intent to purchase the property

Explanation: An earnest money deposit is made by the buyer to demonstrate their serious interest in and commitment to completing the real estate transaction. It is typically held in an escrow account and applied to the purchase price at closing. The deposit shows the seller that the buyer is acting in good faith.

Question 6: Which scenario best illustrates the concept of dual agency in real estate?

[A] An agent representing both the buyer and the seller in the same transaction

[B] Two agents from the same brokerage representing the buyer and the seller

[C] An agent representing two buyers interested in the same property

[D] A broker listing a property while also seeking buyers independently

Correct Answer: [A] An agent representing both the buyer and the seller in the same transaction

Explanation: Dual agency occurs when a real estate agent or broker represents both parties in a transaction, the buyer and the seller. This situation requires clear disclosure and consent from both parties due to the potential for conflicts of interest. Dual agency can also refer to when two agents from the same brokerage represent the buyer and the seller, but the strictest definition involves a single agent representing both sides.

Question 7: What is the primary legal concern associated with verbal agreements in real estate transactions?

[A] They are easier to enforce than written contracts

[B] They are considered legally binding in all 50 states

[C] They may not be enforceable due to the Statute of Frauds

[D] They require less consideration than written agreements

Correct Answer: [C] They may not be enforceable due to the Statute of Frauds

Explanation: The Statute of Frauds is a legal doctrine that requires certain contracts, including those for the sale of real estate, to be in writing to be enforceable. Verbal agreements related to the sale of real property may not be enforceable because they do not meet the written requirement set forth by the Statute of Frauds, making it a significant legal concern in real estate transactions.

CONCLUSION

Congratulations on completing this book! You've just taken a significant leap toward your goal of becoming a licensed real estate professional. By working through this guide, you've demonstrated not only dedication and resilience but also a deep commitment to mastering the complexities of real estate.

I'm thrilled to have been part of your journey to this point. Remember, passing the real estate licensing exam isn't just about acquiring a license; it's about laying the foundation for a successful and fulfilling career in the real estate industry. You've equipped yourself with the knowledge and skills necessary to excel, and I have no doubt that you'll bring great value and integrity to the field.

As you move forward, continue to reflect on the lessons and strategies you've learned here. The practices, insights, and understanding you've gained are tools that will remain relevant throughout your career. The real estate market is dynamic and ever-evolving, and your ability to adapt and grow with it will define your path forward.

Now, as you prepare to take your exam, do so with confidence. You've prepared well, you understand the material, and you're ready to succeed. This is your moment to shine, to demonstrate all that you've learned, and to step confidently into your future as a real estate professional.

Thank you for trusting this guide to prepare you for one of the most important steps in your career. I'm excited for what the future holds for you in real estate. Go forward, take that exam, and ace it—on your very first try!

Here's to your success, your future, and your career. Let's ace this together!

DEAR READER...

As we turn the final page of this book, I want to take a moment to reflect on the journey we've shared and express my gratitude for allowing me to be a part of your path to becoming a real estate professional.

Writing this book has been both a privilege and a profound responsibility. The process involved countless hours of research, writing, and revision, all with the sole aim of providing you with the most accurate, useful, and accessible guide to passing your real estate licensing exam. My goal was to simplify complex topics, clarify the often-confusing aspects of real estate law and practice, and offer you a reliable companion on your way to success.

The creation of this book was driven by a commitment to excellence and a deep desire to empower aspiring real estate professionals like yourself. Each chapter was crafted with care, every question meticulously explained, and all strategies thoroughly tested to ensure that you receive the best preparation possible.

If you found value in your journey through this book, and if it has helped you in any way, I kindly ask you to consider leaving sincere feedback on Amazon. Your insights and experiences are incredibly valuable—not only to me as an author looking to grow and improve, but also to fellow readers who are on similar paths to yours. Your feedback can help spread the message of this book and enable it to reach as many potential real estate professionals as possible.

Thank you once again for choosing this guide. It has been an honor to accompany you on this part of your educational journey, and I look forward to possibly serving you again in the future. Remember, the world of real estate offers endless opportunities for growth, learning, and success. Continue to seek knowledge, strive for excellence, and build your professional network. Your future is bright, and your potential is limitless.

<u>Scan the QR Code below to leave a review of this book</u>

Regards,

Leo Mills

SCAN THE
QR CODE
TO DOWNLOAD
YOUR BONUSES

Made in United States
Orlando, FL
30 June 2025

62483434R00059